MY JOURNEY BACK TO THE SHACK

MY JOURNEY BACK TO THE SHACK

A STORY OF WHO GOD IS AND WHAT HE CAN DO IN A HUMAN HEART.

JOANNE BAIN

Photo credits to Douglas Campbell
Scripture quotations taken from The Holy Bible, New International Version® NIV®
Copyright © 1973 1978 1984 2011 by Biblica, Inc. ™ Used by permission. All rights reserved worldwide.

Scripture quotations are from The Passion Translation®. Copyright © 2017, 2018, 2020 by Passion & Fire Ministries, Inc. Used by permission. All rights reserved. ThePassionTranslation.com.

Goodness of God, from the Victory Album Bethel Music. Written by Jenn Johnson, Jason Ingram, Ben Fielding, Ed Cash, Brian Johnson

ACKNOWLEDGMENTS

To my amazing family, thanks for coming along on the ride as I wrote my book. Through the tears and laughter, you kept me focused with the never-ending cups of tea!! I am who I am today because of your love and support, you have been my biggest cheerleaders.

 Big shout out to Wendy for the hours and hours of editing and for your continued encouragement to get this book to the finishing point, I am forever grateful! Derry, thank you for your expert eye and answering the call to help! It is great to be in touch with you again. Denise, you got it to the finish line, thank you! And to all my friends who danced in the rain with me through the storms of life, I love doing life with you all!!

CONTENTS

CHAPTER ONE - Back to the Beginning

CHAPTER TWO – Life Is a Rollercoaster You Just Got to Ride It

CHAPTER THREE – Church Versus the World?

CHAPTER FOUR – My Knight in Shining Armour

CHAPTER FIVE – The Orkney Days

CHAPTER SIX – Family

CHAPTER SEVEN – Full Steam Ahead

CHAPTER EIGHT – The School Gates

CHAPTER NINE – The Farmhouse

CHAPTER TEN – A Mothers Heart

CHAPTER ELEVEN – The Year the World Stopped

CHAPTER TWELVE – Back to the Shack!

The Journey....

We are all on a journey!! This is like a statement from the start of a motivational speech or an inspirational plaque and those who know me will know I love them!! My house is home to many a deep-felt inspirational thought, positive quote or declaration of hope featured on many of my walls to encourage and motivate daily.

The core of who I am is to encourage and motivate. When my youngest daughter played football, I was always known for giving a motivational chant. I knew nothing about the workings of the game, but I did know how to encourage but it sounded nothing like the usual football chat or language used. I would be encouraging the girls and saying, "Well done! You're doing great"; as one of the other mums would explain, "They're offside Joanne!" Not so great! I didn't understand the rules of the game or see the girls' mistakes; I just wanted to cheer them on. I was often left thinking what happened there?! As I looked to the other mums for a debrief as to why they were all shouting "Are you blind ref?" Football and I have a love hate relationship; the people I love play it; I hate watching it!!!

As a swimming teacher my shouts of encouragement have left pupils in fits of laughter as I passionately teach from the side of the pool. This has often included singing and dancing just to get the best out of the class. or at times I would spend hours in the water alongside them as an extra level of support so they are not doing it on their own, because "You have got this", is much better received if you are side by side.

The further along I travel on this journey of life the more I realise it takes more than declaring positivity, words of encouragement or as a woman of faith, repeating scriptures that God has placed on my heart over the years, truths that I know to be true. Although this has been deeply encouraging and got me through many a dark day, the cry of my heart to God is "there must me more than this".

Life is full of ups and downs, and I believe inside all of us we have a story to tell, to inspire, encourage and learn from, we can also have some laughs along the way. Being a wife and a mother of five, I have many life stories to share, the highs and lows of a life lived underpinned by my relationship and faith in God. This is the driving force behind the woman I am. Life stories of who God is to me in the everyday mundaneness and how he never ever fails to surprise me when he shows up in the detail of my life.

In these pages as I write down my journey of who my God is. Through the journey he has taken me on and with complete transparency to all areas of my life, it is my prayer that you will meet with the Jesus who caught my heart as a 13-year-old girl and became my best friend and my place of refuge, maybe for the first time, or reconnect with him as you to have uttered those words, "There must be more than this!"

 Buckle up as I open my heart and life to share with you my journey that led me back to the shack!!

CHAPTER 1

BACK TO THE BEGINNING

Like all good stories, we must first head back to the beginning to understand where we are going. Growing up in a small seaside village called Inver was just the best. Memories of long hot summers and very cold snowy winters still to this day can fill my dreams. We were a family of four I had an older brother - I spent most of my life trying to get him to at least like me or even tolerate me in the same room. I was a very bubbly child and always talking so probably annoyed him greatly. He was two years older than me and wiser.... or so he thought. Although Christmas and summer holidays were the two occasions where he would let his guard down and we became the best of friends, and I treasured those times. Holidays abroad were something we both got to experience from a young age. I was five years old when I went on an aeroplane for the first time and headed to Romania. During our summer holidays was when my brother was at his best, no striving needed to get him to hang out and play with me. For two weeks of the year, the rules of engagements were relaxed, and all was well with my world. Christmas eve was again a time when it was me and him caught up in the excitement of the magic of the season, that was until the year I desperately wanted a horse (like most young girls) and living in the village surrounded by fields this was not an unrealistic ask. However, this year my brother got a motorbike, and I got a desk!!! Devastation filled my heart, but not to be ungrateful as Santa would be watching, I gushed over my new desk. There are key moments in my life where things have happened that I can look back and laugh at, which I have at this story many times, even my own children can tell this story as they have heard it so often.

My parents are amazing and loved my brother and myself well. We had an amazing childhood and by no means did they ever mean to cause a chink on my little heart that would be the source of belief that would start to shape the thought process of who I was. Questions like, does my brother hate me? Do my parents like him more? Experience of behaviour or circumstance backed up by an emotion or feeling that would reinforce the thought, "is something wrong with me?"

Life in the village of Inver was joyful, our home was a place of many a party and social gathering, and probably where my love for the fun of house gatherings started. My father played football so did my brother, which in turn led to my dad managing teams. As well as the social side my life growing up was always built around football. Throughout my story you will begin to see my love hate relationship with the game. All my weekends were shaped around the towns and villages where dad was playing football. On the plus side, after dropping the boys off, mum and I would head off enjoying time together wandering in and out of the various shops and heading to the local café for something yummy. Then racing back to catch the end of the game to cheer the team on! I always remember the occasion Mum was working and my brother was left in charge. The car was parked and looked out onto the football pitch where dad was playing. I headed off to find some other children to play with, I later returned to the car to find my brother had stripped the car radio and was beginning to put it back together! I was horrified and said, "Dad is going to kill you". As calm as you like my brother said "He will never know. I do it all the time!!" The game was now finished, and the men headed to get changed. As I sat silently, I could hear the pounding of my heart as my brother raced to get the radio back together. He did it with minutes to spare, with a glance in my direction to let me know, if I told I would be dead meat!! Dad jumped into the car completely oblivious of the minor heart attack I had just had. You will not be surprised to learn that my brother got an apprenticeship to become an electrical engineer with the Ministry of Defence at the age of 16!

The drive home listening to the football scores coming across the radio is another memory that even to this day brings flash backs of the car sick feeling triggered by the annoying drone of the voice reading out the results. The highlight was always the exciting prospect of dad calling in at the pub on the way home for a bar supper. It was the icing on the cake when I heard the indicator and I quietly thought, yes!! This was my heart's desire, to spend time as a family and us all to be together. The opposite was also true if you saw the pub getting closer but did not feel the slowing of the car, straight home was where we were headed. Mum and dad would be heading out and we would be left with the babysitter for the evening. Another part of the footballing lifestyle I hated. At other times after a local game, I remember dad being dropped off at the pub with his football mates and mum taking us home. It would be late on by the time he would get back and I would always feel my mum's tension, and I would worry silently alongside her. From a young age I was very in tune with how my mum felt, I seemed to be aware of even the slightest change in her mood and took it upon myself to be the one to help. This all fuelled my thinking around the football culture, and it brought my young heart great stress.

The car journeys with my brother were always a challenge back in the days before seatbelts were a thing. We would fight over who would sit in the middle as you could lean forward resting on the two front seats and hear the radio or mum and dads chat better. He always won and I was left out in the back as the three of them chatted away. It was also the place where my brother would enlighten me on the fact that I should stop singing as he claimed I could not and sounded awful! I was gutted as I loved to sing!!!! Now a parent myself I better understand the challenge of siblings in the back seat of a car. At least these days children are strapped in, as I remember the time my brother came up behind my dad's seat while he was driving and placed his hands over his eyes and said guess who!!! Let's just say there was lots of screaming and my brother never did it again! All this interaction with my brother was perfectly normal sibling behaviour, but in my young sensitive heart this was another action backed up by emotion that shaped some new negative beliefs about myself.

Inver School was where I would spend my primary years, I loved it..... Well mostly. I was a social butterfly, loved my friends, break time and playing netball. Our little village school had the head teachers' house attached to it and I would always volunteer to play in the garden with his children at break time. Even as a young girl the nurturer in me shone through, as I loved looking after young children especially babies. I would often be out pushing the prams of the younger children in the village. Happy to help, I'd go knocking on the doors of the young mums offering my services.

It wasn't long before my struggle with the academic side of school started to become apparent. With our little school growing in number my year group had to be split, a straight class and a mixed class with a lower year. I remember my mum being upset as I was placed in the lower age mixed class. It was not something I was aware of as being a problem, but I remember being taken out of class and going through some testing to see why there was a delay in my development. At this point it was obvious my grasp of spelling was terrible. I was completely different to my brother who sailed through his work and was in all the top groups. Homework became something of a dread and would often end in meltdowns by me. Having to do the spelling drills and read out how to spell the words had my stomach in knots and my mind would go completely blank. I have a very vivid memory of the time I had to spell 'because'. My teacher was infuriated with me and I still think to this day he thought I was making it up and acting the fool, but I really could not get my brain around spelling the word! Notes were sent home in the dreaded homework book and my mum would pick up on the annoyance of the teacher and she took it upon herself to teach me. But after a very heated evening and a lot of tears I was sent to my bath to calm down. I remember later sitting at the feet of my mum as she was brushing my wet hair telling me, "Don't worry you will eventually get it".

Again, my little heart echoed "What is wrong with me?" I do remember the day I learnt to spell "because"; I rushed to tell my teacher who by this point had long given up. His reaction did not fit my excitement for finally grasping it. As the class had moved on the gap in my learning journey was getting bigger. In my young heart foundations of disappointment and a sense of no matter what I do it's never enough had begun to take root.

Primary seven was the best and being head of the school, I thrived. As the school year came to an end, I was involved in the idea that we should write a song to sing to all the parents and teachers at the end of the school assembly in the village hall. All the p7s would meet up and write the song together the whole thing was a surprise for the teachers. It was a huge success!!! Not a dry eye as we sang and celebrated our time at Inver primary. Not bad for a girl whose brother thought she couldn't sing!!

During my years in Primary school, I became aware I think for the first time that there was a God I never questioned that there wasn't it was just a given in my thinking. I recall the visiting ministers, and my first ever memory of church when a friend took me to Sunday school in the tiny village church. I remember sitting and learning about Peter and John and the lame man I was intrigued and was given a little workbook to go along with the story. Something in my little heart grasped this and I was so eager to learn I remember asking for extra work as I wanted to know more. The teacher said she didn't have any other workbooks with her, but I was to ask my mum if I was allowed to call past her house the next day and she would have some ready for me. I was so excited at the new experience of being able to understand the work clearly as normally the written side of learning was a real challenge for me, but it was as if for the first time the lights in my brain were turned on. So, with this I rushed home to tell my mum how the Sunday school teacher had extra work for me, and could I go past tomorrow to pick it up? Now looking back, as a mum myself I now understand her reaction, given my history with homework, the meltdowns that surrounded it and my grasp of learning. But my excitement of what had just happened in Sunday school the feeling of the lights in my brain going on, did not translate well to my poor mum. She misunderstood and just heard 'extra work'. She got angry and told me I had enough work to do at school and that I didn't need any extra from Sunday school as well. She would go and speak to the Sunday school teacher and tell her I would not be back!!! I was disappointed but it made sense and reinforced to me that I struggled and extra work would not be good, so I brushed it aside and carried on with the way things were.

The transition in to Tain Royal Academy was exciting and terrifying all at the same time. It involved getting a bus from the village and travelling the five-mile trip into the local town. Wearing a uniform was also a novelty as at our wee primary school we got to wear what we wanted. Our tie was a black and gold stripe worn with a white shirt and black skirt. First year was a blast!! I loved the new friendships and subjects at school, the moving around between classes and the joys of getting to go down the town for lunch. Travelling on the bus though was very nerve wracking.

One weekend my brother told me that I needed to shave my legs as I was being made fun of by people on the bus, I was horrified!! For one, I didn't know I needed to shave my legs, and two, the horrific idea that people were commenting on it. I later asked my mum about shaving my legs, she informed me I was far too young and not to do it as she was a lot older when she started shaving her legs!! Not satisfied with her answer I headed over to my friend's house to ask her, she said she was already shaving hers; she had an older sister and was very matter of a fact about it. So, given all the evidence I decided that the legs needed shaving!! As the idea that people were making fun of me was way too much!! Delighted to be back on the bus that Monday morning with hair free legs, I was disappointed when no one commented!! When I brought this up with my brother that I had indeed shaved my legs, I asked if anyone noticed, he started howling and laughing and said "Don't be daft I only told you so you wouldn't be made fun off!!!" I was so annoyed at him as he had no idea of the dilemma he had put me in. Looking back, what a great big brother for looking out for me. Why tell you this story? Well, it's an insight into how I processed life, when presented with a problem, I would ask questions, sometimes a lot of questions!! And also, how I misunderstood my brother's heart to help me and to avoid getting made fun of!!

The school bus was now not such a scary place as I settled in and enjoyed it; I made more friends, not just in my year but out with my age group because of being on the bus. I loved hanging out with the older girls and being upstairs in the bus laughing and chatting away after school, it was a great way to end a day. I learnt to move freely between age groups and feel comfortable chatting away. There was one time when the vibes on the bus were not great, my stomach was churning, I had no idea what was going on I just knew there was a bad atmosphere and I did not like it!! So, I started asking around and eventually someone told me that there was going to be a fight. And to my horror I heard the boy that was known for always being in trouble had some beef with my brother!! I felt sick! I desperately tried to get to the bottom of it, but no one knew or was not willing to tell. This went on for around a week, the sick feeling would catch me as I would be chatting to the older girls on the bus desperately asking them to tell this older boy to back off and that my brother did not want a fight. These girls did not seem as concerned as I was, to them it was gossip and the tension on the bus was exciting. It was killing me!! As the week went on, I had talked myself into thinking it would be ok, it was all talk. Then one day walking home there seemed to be a crowd of people following us, in my head I was keeping myself calm and saying, "Just keep walking, we are nearly home". As we turned the corner, and the house was up ahead, a friend of my brother's put his arm around me; I felt comforted and was able to calm the scared feeling momentarily as he directed me forward. I though he was helping me, but he was distracting me, getting the little sister out the way. A group of boys jumped my brother and started beating him up! As I turned and saw this I started screaming and running down the street. My screams were so loud the neighbours came out as I was yelling "Please help my brother!!" I was taken in a couple of doors down from my house as some other people helped my brother. I was with the neighbours for some time, they calmed me down and told me my parents had been called and they were on their way home from work. These lovely people spent time with me and made me feel safe again and kept reassuring me my brother was fine, my parents were with him. I had dinner with this family and as we chatted around their table, I could feel myself relax. When mum came to pick me up later, with the rush of emotion at seeing her I started crying again. "Don't cry he is fine, let's get you home!!" she said. Years later I learned my dad went to each of the boys involved; he knocked on the doors of my brother's so-called friends and confronted them. It was just after this my parents made the decision to put the house up for sale, and so we left the village of Inver and moved into Tain.

Chapter 2

LIFE IS A ROLLERCOASTER YOU JUST GOT TO RIDE IT!!!

After moving into Tain it took me a while to forgive my mum and dad as Inver was a precious place to grow up in and will always hold a special place in my heart. Although I had not realised at the time the reasons for moving, I soon started to enjoy the benefits of living right next door to the Academy, rolling out of bed and running up to the school just as the bell rang. No more school bus, my God parents lived in Tain, and their house was a special place for me, so the idea of walking to their house to visit anytime filled my heart with delight. I embraced school life, the friends, the teachers good and bad all made for an interesting roller coaster ride. My academic work was not the best, but my cheery bubbly attitude and the fun to be found kept me going. But the girl drama stressed me out! My emotions would get the better of me, fall outs would be had and I was always left feeling it was my fault regardless of whether it was or not. When I was 13 years old my mum and God mum dropped me off at a holiday camp for the day. I was horrified, I had no idea why they would do this to me, and I just wanted to hang out with them. This would be an event that would change my life! Over the week, these amazing people full of love and joy scooped me up and took me on a journey to discovering Jesus. I felt safe, I really enjoyed the fun activities, they even did singing and this just delighted my heart as I loved to sing. I could feel myself being sucked along in this wave of love. With it being on for the whole day, we got to eat our meals around big tables laughing and chatting together. I am sure this is where my love for this kind of thing was birthed and it continues in my life even to this day.

At the end of the day there was always a chat, talking about God and stories from the Bible. I can't say I listened much, but I was just so happy, I felt safe, loved, and joy filled my heart, so I was happy. Towards the end of the week one of the team told a story about a man called Jesus and that He is standing at the door of your heart. They showed a picture of this, and it caught my attention, as I looked at this picture and heard the words, "He is standing knocking at the door of your heart and there is no door handle at his side you must open it, he can't do it." My young heart leapt instantly, I said to myself, "Oh my goodness, come in, I didn't know." This is the moment my life changed forever as the love of Jesus caught this young heart and filled it with love and protected it for the roads of life that lay ahead.

I remember being 14 and in my eyes this was the worst year of my life!! I have a dramatic flair and it's never far away when describing my feelings!! Everyone was older than me in my class and they were allowed to go to the local town hall when the bands played. I used to beg to go but until I turned 15 that was not going to happen. I would huff and puff my way around the house declaring things to be very unfair and find myself sulking, but then later wondering what on earth I was doing as I was now in this stinker of a mood which I would find it hard to climb out of. Emotions for me took on a whole new meaning with the teenager in me now fully alive. It was hard to find the bubbly personality which was the truth of who I was. The rollercoaster that was life had me screaming with joy on one hand and screaming, "Get me off" on the other!

As I navigated the hard work in the Academy that was getting increasingly more difficult my brain was finding it hard to cope. I remember having to study the book 'Shane' for English, it was awful! I hated every minute of it! I really struggled to read at the best of times, but this book was so boring, I remember begging my mum to read it for me and tell me what it was about. Week after week passed, and I was found crying out "I don't want to read it!!" Not only had I to read it but I had to write a report on it as well! Sunday night would roll round, and it filled me with dread yet again the chapters needed reading for school on Monday, I was using my dramatic flair to announce "I don't know why I am having to read this, what good is it going to do me in life learning about a cowboy!!!" But eventually I finished it, handed in the essay and was glad to see the back of it!!!

The dramatic side to my character was a great way to express my feelings. One of my best friends was involved in the local drama group and encouraged me to come along to the auditions for the Christmas pantomime held in the local Town hall. I jumped at the chance and headed along, although put in this very public setting I suddenly became very shy. There was a large turnout for auditions, we were all put in groups of four, and we had to walk out on to the large stage, read some lines from a script, and sing a song together and then a few lines singing solo. On this occasion I was cast in the chorus, my best friend got one of the lead roles; she was amazingly confident and could sing beautifully. And so would begin another inner battle. Not only was my brother better and mum and dad liked him better and now my friend was better!! I started to feel very insecure about myself, as my journey of comparison had begun. With an already fragile heart I began to draw conclusions from emotions, backed by what it looked like; I was not as good as I did not get a part, she did so she was better. This was all an inner battle, but with my heart that was now open to the love of Jesus I asked Him a lot of questions and this became my dialogue and conversations with Him on the inside of me.

The years I was involved in the pantomime were just fab. I did go on and have lead roles in later years and this really helped my confidence, I loved every minute, the rehearsals, the singing, the tight bond of the cast, and still to this day we have a family tradition to head to a pantomime together!! And although I love it, I say every year to the family "I would have enjoyed it more if I had been in it!!"

Having now begun this journey with opening the door to Jesus, I remember being so delighted with the joy and love I felt in my heart, I could not even put words to it. The team from the holiday club had told me at the time that it was good to tell someone what I had done, as it made it all the more exciting when you share. So, I had gone rushing home to tell my mum, I burst into the living room (remember drama is my thing!!!), announcing with great joy and delight "I gave my heart to Jesus tonight!!" Mum looked stunned; I picked up on her shock and thought she was not happy. However later discovered three weeks previous she also had given her heart to Jesus and at the time she had also asked God for a friend to walk this out with, I am just not sure she expected it to be me! I started going along to the local Church of Scotland with my mum and God mum. Let's just say it was a bit of a culture shock! It was no holiday club with the joyful laughing people, the fun games and happy clappy songs!! No, it was church pews, an old organ and a pulpit that seemed to be way up high. And the man I had met at the holiday camp was now wearing robes and a white collar round his neck, he also looked very serious. But I knew what had happened in my heart at the holiday club was very real, so if this was church, I was all in!! Over the years I got to know the people and I loved them, their gentle hearts made me feel safe. I was the youngest in the congregation and all my friends were forty plus. This added in an interesting dynamic to my life as I was a teenager highly emotional and very dramatic. This rollercoaster ride of my life just added in a few new loop de loops!!

Reading the bible was a minefield for me, with the added pressure that reading was definitely not my thing. I do remember the time I was sitting on my bed, and I said "God you are going to have to help me as I have no idea and don't understand?" I was flicking through and came across the book of Jeremiah my eyes fell on verse 11 in chapter 29; I know the plans I have for you says the Lord plans to prosper you not to harm you.....This was a defining moment in my life it was like a hug on the inside when I came to the realisation that God knows me and has a plan for my life. It was a huge relief as I had no idea what I wanted to do with my life!!

Attending career advice meetings in the school always left me feeling deflated as I had no idea what my future held in terms of a career. With my grades not being the best, the job list they gave me filled me with a sense of failure. None of the jobs listed even came close to what I thought I might want to do. This is when I would remember the verse, I know the plans I have for you!! It would give me a sense of hope and remind me that I was not a lost cause. God had a plan, with his help I would be able to work out what that was. I had an amazing biology teacher who suggested I would make a great nurse. I had no idea what I needed to become a nurse, but words spoken in encouragement gripped my heart and I thought, "Wow he sees that in me", I tucked that idea in the back of my mind and would explore it at a later date.

The bible talks about a man making his plans, but God directing his steps. This is found in Proverbs 16 verse 9. I believe this to be true of my mum and dads' choice of Godparents, as God was not part of our life back in the day when my parents made this decision. The two families were close, and we often joked about what it would be like to all live together.

Having Godparents in the town was just the best as this was, next to my own house, the best place to hang out. Mum and dad both worked full-time so in the summer holidays my Godmum looked after my brother and me. They were mum and dad's best friends who in turn were Godparents to their children, who were much younger than us. So, to get to spend the summer holidays with them thrilled my heart. Another opportunity to help with the children, changing nappies out for walks pushing the buggy. I would love it when we got to bake and my favourite of all was when we made toffee!! I remember seeing her cleaning the toilet and I was horrified she had her hand inside the pan. Dramatically I announced I could never do this!! She said "Jojo" (this is what everyone called me) "you can do anything with a pair of rubber gloves." When I became a student nurse years later and was faced with some disgusting jobs, I would hear her voice in my head, and I would give a little smile and reach for the gloves. The house was always busy with many of the local mums meeting for coffee and I loved it, more children to play with! This amazing lady was also a sounding board for me; we talked a lot about a range of subjects. She would listen to me as I chatted away and she always made me feel heard, her reactions towards me made me feel safe. She was also good at reining me in. Many a time she would be sitting next to me and I would feel a gently poke on my leg if I began to get a bit loud and over excited. It was never discussed but it caught me and brought me back to earth if my chatting or conversation was heading off topic. This continued into adulthood as I remember not that long ago when Katie, my daughter, had introduced her new boyfriend to the family. We were all round the table and I was quizzing this young man and basically giving him a hard time, I felt this nip on my leg and it caught my attention. No words were spoken but it worked in pulling my focus back on track. Mum and dad's choice of Godparents was no accident, a choice that directed us all on a journey, especially for me as my Godmum has played a vital role in helping me over the years. She was the daughter of a shepherd and as I look back over the years, she became the Shepherd in my life, a gentle voice of calm and now and again the tap of the shepherd's crook in the form of a wee nip on the leg to keep me in check.

We all have people in our lives that influence us, and I believe God directs people into our path. Handpicked by Him my Godmum is one of many who God has used to shape my life and to see Him in His people. The daughter of a shepherd in the natural but in God's kingdom she was the daughter of the ultimate Shepherd Jesus!! She lives her life out quietly and gently shepherding the people God sends her way, and I will be forever grateful to God for bringing us all together and for the journey we share and the love that is between us all.

My own mum is also key in the woman I have become, her knowledge and understanding of the bible inspires me greatly!! Over time Mum and I had come to realise there were not many opportunities for young people in church life, I remember being curious about a scripture that talked about setting a room aside, found in 2 Kings chapter 8. As I discussed it with mum, we decided we would make our home available for young folk to hang out in, as well as with the now growing number of younger members of the church. It also became a place where I would take my friends from school, our house was at the bottom of the playing fields, a group of us would run all the way at break time, put the kettle on and have tea and digestive biscuits, and we'd just hang out and have a laugh. We then would belt it back through the field before the bell rang!! We became experts at timing it perfectly. My own house all these years later is still a place where the kettle is always on and many a conversation sorting the world out happens as we travel through this roller coaster of life. Even after I left home my parents still had an open door and many young people would call in, mum ran a bible study on a Sunday morning and tea and toast was served as young people came around her table as she taught them.

I was now in sixth year, I stayed on at school because I was still trying to work out what I wanted to do, and not because I was loving the studying!! It was challenging in many ways, I was really struggling with my self- worth on the inside and my friendship group had taken a turn. There had been a fall out, and not many people were speaking to me. I remember trying to sort this out, by asking questions to get to the bottom of what was going on, I was so broken on the inside and just wanted it all sorted!! It was killing me!! I had managed to navigate my way through, although it was a lonely year, I found that if I did a pre nursing course I would be able to get the qualifications needed to do nursing. So, I applied and was accepted into the pre nursing course at Thurso College. It was such a relief, now I could leave school and that which had become a daily torture for me, with behaviour from friends backed up by my emotions, I knew I had developed an unhealthy thought pattern about myself. The day I finally got to leave school I went around and got all my teachers to sign my leaver's form, which was lovely as I was able to say goodbye to them. I got to the last class which was maths, a place of torture. I had really struggled with this subject; it was the class I felt most lonely in as the friends that weren't speaking to me were also in it at this time. So, I walked up the corridor, went to the toilet to pull myself together and talked myself out of crying. I was praying in my head the whole time and finally, I took a deep breath and knocked on the door. The class went silent. I was amazed, my voice was calm and the words that came out made sense, no one would have known what was going on on the inside of me. The teacher was lovely and wished me well as I turned and walked out of the classroom. I had to hold myself back from running as the silent stares from them, the people I had gone through almost six years of school with said nothing. My heart was breaking; it was the prayers in my heart that got me out of that classroom without bursting into tears. I made my way to the head teacher's office, one last signature and then I could walk out of Tain Royal Academy and never return. As I sat waiting outside his office until he was free, I looked around at the lovely ladies in the office and the sick room, which I knew well over my time here due to ongoing painful periods that had me passing out on occasion. I sat and contemplated my time here, it was not all bad. I had in the most part loved it and have many happy fun memories. My heart was in pain, but I knew I would have to deal with it, I asked God, "Please get me through this last part without crying." The head teacher was ready to see me, I did really like the him, and he carried a real sense of authority while also being approachable. We chatted and he asked me my plans, he said it was a pleasure having me in his school, he spoke about my bubbly personality and how nursing would suit me. He signed off my form and handed it to me saying, "It's so good that as a school we can support young people in their journeys, even if it's not in an academic way, until they realise what it is they want to do." He wished me well and I left. His words ringing in my ears. I walked home with a heart that was in pain and emotions that were all over the place. I had processed in my heart that that was a negative response from the head teacher and that I should not have stayed on in sixth year. My own insecurities misunderstood what he meant. But as I look back, what he said was actually key, and in schools today we could learn a lot from this head teacher, the academic side of school is a struggle for many but it's about supporting young people until they work out the path they will take. We cannot all be measured by our exam results. The pain of the day I poured into my journal, and I knew forgiveness was key to healing the pain but needed to get it out first. As I wrote the words, I would feel the storm in my heart calming, the key to forgiveness is letting go of the pain and handing it over to the one who took the greatest pain of all for us, Jesus!! I asked for forgiveness for my part in the breakdown of the friendships and asked Jesus to help me forgive them for their part. As I closed my journal, I knew I was leaving it with Him.

Life was full of ups and downs, and with my newfound love in my heart and faith in who God was, I was able to navigate my way through life.

Now in Thurso studying, hanging out with my newfound friends, enjoying the summer weather (probably a little too much), I had been badly burnt on the back of my legs. I had fallen asleep in the sun!! I was in so much pain I needed to go to the doctors and had to return home for the weekend. This was the same weekend that a lady in our church who was a teacher in one of the surrounding small schools, had suffered a horrible attack. I don't remember much of the details, but she had been taken hostage for several hours, until eventually she was rescued by the police. I was so scared when I heard this story, but for some reason I volunteered to stay with her at her house as she lived alone. I could not bear the idea of her being scared and being on her own so, it was decided I would sleep over to keep her company. This was all well and good until it came to bedtime. I could feel the nerves on the inside of me as the darkness was closing in. I started to get scared, thinking what I would do if someone came into the house, after all bad things do happen!! She headed off to her bed and I was now on my own, I was terrified and in a lot of pain with my legs. I started praying!! A friend of mine had taught me a new way of praying (which I will explain later), so this became my dialogue all night. I lay awake most off the night praying protection over us both and praying she slept well, along with please help my legs! It was a long night, and I was ever so glad when morning came around and I was relieved to hear she had slept well. As we spent the day together, she voiced she would be fine being on her own now and thanked me for keeping her company. I was so relieved and thankful that prayer works and I was glad to get back to my own bed, and to get my mum to help put the cream on my legs as I was in agony, they were on fire!!

When living up in Thurso and struggling with the concept of being away from home, the voice of my mum on the phone would calm me down I phoned her most days we just talked general chit chat, but these conversations helped bring the peace and safety back to my heart. My God mum without fail sent me a handwritten letter every week!! There was always a bar of chocolate in the envelope. These letters were such a comfort; the days they would arrive I physically felt the hug and love in my heart, bringing peace in the roller coaster of my life. An inspirational quote would say it's the little things in life that make the difference; I can say for sure it definitely is.

Chapter 3

CHURCH VERSUS THE WORLD?

Growing up in faith within the Church of Scotland setting has given me a great foundation of the Bible, but although I went week in week out, I never really got the buzz my mum had. She talked about counting down the hours until the next service or prayer meeting; I can't say that was my experience. Our minister was amazing although I'm not quite sure what he made of me, but he had four daughters so was probably more aware of me than I gave him credit for. For me as always, it was the songs that captured my heart. The song numbers would be written out on the boards and displayed up high on the balcony area, that was my excitement for church, I would have them all looked out in the hymn book before the service would start. I'd read over them and would decide if I liked them or not by how the words hit my young heart. Some just didn't make sense to me, others I just loved. Services were only an hour long, so if it was a poor week in the song department I wouldn't have to sit too long, and there was always the evening service so I would think maybe the song choices would be better!! Our church was an amazing building and the smell of a dusty old Church of Scotland still stirs within me a sense of home and safety. Each service was run in the same way. You would hear the buzz of hushed voices as everyone arrived, and then the choir would come in and take their seats at the front of the church beside the organ. This was the cue for people to settle down. The door would open down at the front and the children from the Sunday school would come in and take their seats the minister would follow in his robes and go and sit up in his pulpit. Silence had now settled in the sanctuary as we would wait for him to pray before taking his place in front of the lectern to welcome us. The children's talk was always fun, and our minister adopted a warm friendly approach for addressing them, and there was always a joyful children's song to sing. Many of them I could sing word for word even to this day, as they are etched on my heart. As I am typing, the song, One More Step along the World I Go, is buzzing around in my head. After the children left to head up to the hall the sombre serious mood would fall in the atmosphere of the church. Well this is how I sensed it. We would get on with the intercession prayer, where the minister would pray for matters of local and world concern. I'd often get lost in my own thoughts and feel myself drift off to sleep only to be dragged back by the sudden jolt of my head as it would fall forward! With a quick check to see if anyone had noticed as I would feel guilty again. Years later, I now realise God loves my thoughts, He knows them, and nothing is hidden from Him. When the service was over and the organ began to play a joyful tune, the buzz of voices and people moving around would bring the place back to life. I loved the chat with everyone after the service and I would love going in search of some of my favourite people to catch up with. Our minister stood waiting at the door on the way out and shook our hands as we left. I'd head home after with my mum and God mum, our house was the nearest, so we would arrive there after the service to have a cuppa and a catch up. I enjoyed this the most about a Sunday, with my dad and God dad coming in from the golf, some of our best family times were spent on a Sunday going for country walks together and enjoying food. Summer BBQs were a must, with many happy memories of long lazy Sundays and two families' together enjoying life. But, this for me started a belief that the church and world were seen as two different things, one was right, and one was wrong.

A very significant turning point for me in my Faith journey was when my lovely friends from the church took me to Ayr on a trip to Butlins. This was no ordinary Butlins holiday, the event was called Spring Harvest and it would ignite my passion and love for Jesus even more. We had arrived, there were over 2000 Christians attending this event!! I was buzzing, the atmosphere was electric and that was us just getting checked in! I had no idea what to expect, and as I was taken to the first night session, I thought I was going to burst with excitement!! The stage had a full band, the auditorium was full and when the band started up with the first song and the sound of that many voices coming together was so powerful and it was like all the lights on the inside of me had come on. This was no Church of Scotland service!! As I looked around, I saw young people my age in the hundreds. I remember phoning my mum that evening, my excitement was spilling over as I explained to her "There are people my age here!!!" I would attend this event for the next three years and it became a place where my journey in faith grew. I also made some amazing friends whom I would journey with for a season. These events were held over Easter, so the Sunday before we left, they would have a service. It was here that I'd learn exactly what had happened to Jesus on the cross. I was aware that he had died for me but didn't fully understand the concept. I remember the service very clearly that day. The speaker was describing the cross and the full extent of the torture Jesus suffered hit me when we were all handed a large nail. I held it in my hands and looked at it, the feel of the sharp rusty nail and the words that were being spoken hit my heart. This was driven into my Jesus, in his feet and hands! It was over whelming and took me to a new place in my understanding of what he had done for me. It also took me to a new place when singing. Although it was already a passion of mine, it had now taken on a whole new meaning. I carried that nail in the front of my bible for many years. Spring Harvest would also be the place I would discover communion, and why it was so important to take it!! Back home I had never taken communion as you would have to be a member of the church to take it. So, after returning from Spring Harvest, I planned to seek out my minister and ask to become a member. I had now become the youngest member in our church. My first communion in the church drew attention to the fact that there were huge differences between the way the church service in Tain took communion and the way we took it at Spring Harvest. Looking back now, my heart in the way I took it was always the same, but it added in another level of questions as to why it is so different? The friends I made at Spring Harvest were mostly from Arbroath, so I would travel to see them at weekends heading off on the bus gaining confidence to travel by myself. This brought a new level of freedom to me and I loved it!! It was here I was introduced to the Baptist church and saw my first ever baptism, and true to form this started another new series of questioning. I had been told that because I was christened as a baby I didn't need to be baptised, but something in my heart wanted to know more. The days in Arbroath with this special bunch of young people were a blast!! So much of the happy, funny and outrageous antics still bring a smile to my face today. I will be forever grateful to them for taking this wee highland lass under their wing and showing me that faith could be fun!!!!

Over the years different people came and joined us in Tain Parish Church, and I remember this young adult coming, she was like a breath of fresh air. My parents called her the Killy lass, she was a gift to me for a season as I battled out my teenage years in Tain, and she would also be the one to introduce me to the power of the Holy Spirit. I remember one evening we were hanging out in my bedroom chatting after an evening service, she asked me had I thought much about the Holy Spirit, its power and the gifts. I definitely had not! She informed me that God likes to give us good gifts and we just need to ask. "One way of knowing you have the Holy Spirit is to ask him for the gift of tongues," she explained, "it's a heavenly language that only God understands." I was well up for that as I struggled with the English language as well as the German I had learned at school. So, to speak a language only God understood sounded awesome, plus the fact it was a gift meant I didn't have to learn it, it was just given. So, I asked "What do we need to do?" I was nervous but really excited to start speaking this language. She explained that we just needed to start thanking God for who He was and what His Son had done. This was easy for me, as most of the writings in my journals were this, so now I was able to voice out loud my heart. I remember being less aware of my voice and more aware of this love and a warm feeling that came over me. When I eventually became aware of my voice again, I did not recognise the words and I started roaring and laughing as I couldn't believe I was speaking this language that only God understood. The bible calls it speaking in tongues. This was a very special time for me and became a way of expressing myself to God when my heart had no words. In times of fear and when things felt out of control this became the way I prayed. I will always be grateful to the Killy lass who introduced me to the power of the Holy Spirit.

My experience of faith and church life was expanding, as I drew up conclusions in my head of good and bad experiences, some of them would take root in my heart. I became a very black and white thinker. My heart was sold out to Jesus that was never in doubt, but now a young adult with my sights set on boyfriends and social life the church did not offer much in that department. So, I would be out and about at the weekend enjoying the bands that came to the local town hall whilst dating some of the local boy. I had a blast, but there was always this expectation around church culture that it would be better to be with someone who believed the same as you as the verse 'do not be unequally yoked' was quoted and spoken about in bible class and youth events. I didn't even know what that meant, but I drew the conclusion that you had to marry a

Christian. But with the choice of males in the church being practically non-existent this did not help my dilemma. I did head out to some of the other local churches if they had events on but really, I was scouting out the local talent. Along the way I experienced the Free Church, and again this was quite different. They had no music, just a man that would get up and lead the song from the front. But the sound of all the voices and no music was still something powerful that stirred in my heart, and yes, they had some good-looking boys in the Free Church, so I was always keen to visit if mum suggested it. So, this 'church versus the world' dilemma played a tug of war in my thinking, but my journals were full of conversations and the concerns I would pour out to God in an evening, and He would settle my heart as I was now a young woman who just loved Jesus, so the best place to leave them was with Him.

Before heading off to nursing college, I spent a summer with an organisation call OM (Operation Mobilisation); they were all about equipping and training people to spread the good news of the gospel. This was a summer well spent and I loved every minute of it, even though I had a rocky start. I was feeling very home sick, so I phoned home to mum, and she had a firm chat with me and helped me get my head straight. Phoning my mum was something I was in the habit of doing when I felt scared or vulnerable; it was a routine I had started back in the days when we lived in Inver. I would walk home from school and phone mum at her work to say I was home. So, in a way hearing her voice brought comfort, even on this occasion when she was firm with me it gave me reassurance. We started the training off in Germany and then headed to Belgium to put into practice what we had learned; it was definitely 'out of your comfort zone' stuff. But my most favourite thing was the street evangelism, we got to dress up as fun characters as we did mimes and fun activities for the children and passers-by on the streets of Belgium, my dramatic side got a chance to shine. The team we worked with were amazing; I loved all the different people I met from all over the world. All of us had a passion for Jesus and wanted to grow and learn more ways of how we could share this. While writing this I chuckle to myself that God would bring a man into my life where this would be his passion too. We just have quite different approaches to it, I am more of a 'let me show you who my God is come, do life with me', whereas Ricky is a fantastic communicator and can turn most conversations around so it has a relevance and connection to life and faith.

With the now vast experience of life in churches and around Christians, and looking at it now in 2021, and seeing it's not so much 'church versus the world', but its more 'we are the church to the world' in the conversations we have the lives we lead, in the rough stuff and the good stuff, we should begin to ask ourselves "What is speaking louder to the world?". So, with Jesus, the under pinning absolute rock of it all and as I continue to share my life in total transparency, you will see that in every twist and turn, my journaling is the key, as this is me falling at the feet of Jesus in tears or in rejoicing, in the struggles with the big and small things, you will come to see that He loves to hear from us and bring peace in any situation.

Whilst preparing to move to Thurso, Mum had found out through a friend that a minister and his wife were looking for a lodger, so I headed up to stay in the Free Church manse with them and another girl who was also studying at the college. This was to begin a year of struggling leaving my parents, versus enjoying college life, along with having a blast with this amazing couple who opened their home up to us. We would have great discussions around the church and faith, and they looked after us very well. It also kept me very grounded in my newfound freedom and all the night life Thurso had to offer, which was not much!! But they did have a bowling alley where I discovered that gin and I don't mix! Although not having much experience with alcohol we did have a very funny night, but I later bitterly regretted thinking the gin tasted like lemonade. I have never drunk gin since!!

Completing my course, I was then accepted to train as a nurse at the Royal College of Nursing Aberdeen in 1995. I was so excited and could not wait to get started, mum and dad drove me down and got me settled into the ARI (Aberdeen Royal Infirmary) staff home opposite Foresterhill hospital, and this was to be my home for the next 18 months. I had a small room with a sink in it, and right across the hall was the toilet and a large bathroom with a bath in it. Across the whole of the staff home there were not many baths so to get one right across from me was just a gift, baths are my safe space and a place to contemplate. I've had many a conversation with God as I lay in the bath, a lot of my life's problems would get mulled over with Him. Looking back this does not seem a big deal having a bath in my space, but to me this is God in the detail of my life. ARI staff quarters was now home and as the church versus world struggle still raged on in my mind, after visiting many churches across Aberdeen I concluded that my newfound friends were more of a family to me than the cold welcome I perceived at the time when I visited church. I remember telling my mum this one Sunday evening on the phone after she asked if I had been to church, I told her that my new friends made me more welcome than any of the churches so, no I wouldn't be going to church.

I embraced the life of a nurse and loved every minute of it along with the deep friendships, love for life and the work, it was a great season. I still look back on these days and smile. We were a wild bunch and we laughed a lot!! My first placement was to be up in Elgin in the psychiatric hospital. This was an eye-opening experience as I saw some of the devastating effects that drugs can have on people and the state they were left in. Being quite naive I had never considered drugs but having seen the effects and what could go wrong this left me absolutely convinced I would never take them! Although I did at one point try weed to be cool, it was not cool at all!! I hated it!!! This experience at the psychiatric hospital left me fascinated with how our brains work. If I had not already chosen to do adult nursing, I definitely would have taken this path. During my placement, I was on shift the day the electric shock treatment was being done, and I remember being asked if I was ok to go down with the patients and wait with them before and after their treatment. I was keen to get as much experience as I could out of my time in Elgin, so I jumped at the chance to help. This one experience stands out in my mind. I remember walking down with the patient on the trolly and as we entered the recovery ward, I sensed fear. I started praying in my head as I looked around, no one else seemed afraid, but I could not shrug the feeling. I remember holding the patient's hand and I saw fear in their eyes, I started praying to God in my heart "I have no idea what is going on here Lord," and asking Him, "please be with these patients." I was very glad to get back up to the ward and peace restored in my heart. My time in Elgin came to an end so I headed back down to Aberdeen and was very pleased to be reunited with the gang. Laughter and antics were the life in ARI staff home and boy, if those walls could talk, they would tell some very funny stories!!

Embracing life and the freedom of living in the city my faith was still in me and my heart for Jesus never changed, it was just not always expressed through attending church. The guilt of not reading my bible would catch me unawares sometimes I would see it sitting beside my bed and I would whisper, "Sorry God I know I need to read it," but my feelings of; I am just having so much fun, would have me brushing aside this conviction! My friends in the staff home were all aware of my faith in God; they would see my bible on my bed side (they didn't know I wasn't reading it) which started some great conversations around this. After one of our many discussions they all decided they would like to go to church and see what it's like, so, I invited a group of them to a baptism at Gerard Street Baptist Church one evening. I was absolutely delighted to take them all along to the service. The experience of standing watching the baptism, hearing the music and being with my friends in church was like everything came into alignment and all was well with my world!! Such a special night where my two worlds collided. This added to my ever-increasing questions around 'church versus' the world and why there is such a gap?

CHAPTER 4

MY KNIGHT IN SHINING ARMOUR

They say love is blind, and in my case, this is true!! Thankfully, not when it comes to looks as Ricky's handsome features were definitely a plus!! We met in a nightclub in Aberdeen in March 1996 and my friend was terribly rude to him. I apologised profusely, he then asked me "do you want a drink?" So not to be rude I accepted. He introduced me to his friends who were with him, and they all seemed lovely. This is where the first 'blind' comes in. Some of the guys around the bar were Aberdeen football players, I had not known it at the time, but had I caught wind of this before, I would have been off!! This lifestyle was not for me, I hated the football culture! This encounter that some may call a 'chance' encounter, changed the direction of my life. I truly believe that as we make plans in our heart it's God who determines our steps. I didn't believe this just because I went to church and did and said all the right things, but because my heart was full of the love Jesus had poured into it at the age of 13. There was still the pull in my spirit toward the verse in the book of Jeremiah, of the good plan God has for me which is the underpinning verse of my life. It's at the core of who I am.

About a week after meeting Ricky, I headed to go to Glasgow for the weekend to meet up with some friends. Glasgow remains one of my favourite cities to visit. It's not the beauty of the city but its people, the fun and laughter and just the way they are, and I felt I fitted in!! I had also attended a few churches there in the past and loved the way they did church, so it would have been a big pull for me to move there after completing my training. The whole time I was away I just missed Ricky, so I was relieved to get back up to Aberdeen to see him. Already we had a strong connection. I remember sitting on his sofa in the weeks that followed and holding his hand while watching a movie, as I was looking at his hand, I heard a voice that was so soft saying "he is like your dad, strong, he will look after you!!" Again, I felt the hug on the inside of me; I definitely decided in my heart that night that this was the man for me! I was still very aware of the bible verse 'do not be unequally yoked', so I would have conversations in my heart with God, asking if He would show me if Ricky was the man for me. I would ask Ricky over the coming weeks if he believed in God and what he thought about faith, he would share some of his stories about his time growing up in Orkney, he told about his Boys Brigade leader who would tell stories about Jesus. A group of boys would go to the leader's house and hang out on a Friday night, a guitar would be brought out and they would all sing. This was music to my ears and would also help with unfolding events, as my love blindness had still not considered how involved Ricky was in the football culture. Ricky also challenged me, as when he would see my bible in my room at the staff home, he would pick it up and start asking questions. I'd be straight on the defensive as the guilt pricked at my heart because I had not read it in a while. I asked him if he would call himself a Christian, he said he just didn't know enough about it, but it was definitely something he often thought about. He told me a story of the time he was out with his friends, a little worse for wear with the drink. They were walking down by the harbour where someone was giving out leaflets, his friend took one and almost immediately threw it on the ground, but he picked it up and put it in his pocket unaware of what it was. He told me he took it out and looked at it the next morning and saw the words 'Jesus is your Saviour', written on it along with the OM logo. OM had ships that went around the world, and they were in Aberdeen for the week. I could not believe my ears!! I excitedly announced that I had spent a summer with OM and had spent time on their ships!! This was enough to settle my heart and believe what I felt the night I held his hand and heard the soft voice of God telling me Ricky was my future.

It was time to introduce him to the family. So, we headed up North and now knowing he had sung songs with this boys' group in Orkney I felt confident to share some of my music with him!! I knew Ricky was an Elvis fan, his flat was full of his records and pictures, he had an older taste in music, and I liked it as my brother had been into the heavy rave stuff and I could not cope with that! This was also around the time that Peter Andre released the song 'Mysterious Girl', we loved the tune as it was catchy and fun, we bought the cassette tape for our road trip up North. I also brought some of my church music to introduce to him on our journey. I was so excited to head North, I loved being back in the Highlands and it made my heart sing!! And, I loved a road trip! We chatted and sang along to songs all the way up to Tain. One of the first ever songs I shared with Ricky, was one called 'Teach Me to Dance to the Beat of Your Heart', referring to God's heart. Ricky caught on to the tune quickly as the words were quite repetitive, so we belted it out together, "Teach me to dance to the beat of Your heart, teach me to move in the power of Your spirit, teach me to walk in the light of Your presence, teach me to dance to the beat of Your heart". We hear so often that our words are powerful, and I truly believe they are!! In this happy time of travelling up North, as we sang, we were also declaring truths over our lives as a couple. This would begin the journey of the out workings of our faith. Looking back over the last 25 years with Ricky, just as the words of the song go; I can say that's exactly what God has taught us to do.

As Tain grew closer Ricky became quiet, I could sense his nerves. I told him "Don't worry they are going to love you". And so was the case, he was a huge hit with the family, mum and dad loved him! And sometime later mum said she knew the day she met Ricky he was going to be her son in law. I brought him round to meet my God parents, looking to my God mum and searching her eyes, she looked at me and said, "Good one Jojo!!" Phew, the most important people in my life had seen him as I saw him. The icing on the cake for Ricky and I know he loves to tell this story, was that he was surrounded by footballers and most importantly, Rangers supporters!! On the Sunday before we left to go back to Aberdeen, the Rangers v Celtic match was on and my nana and grandpa from Dingwall were through visiting, and they were watching it! So, for Ricky being in a house full of Ranger's fans it was the cherry on top!! And when he learned about my grandpa being a Ross County legend, he knew he was in with the right family. I was still unaware at this point of just how much the football culture was such a huge part of Ricky's life! Love truly was blind!!

The next few months were a whirl wind, Ricky and I met and married in nine months (and no, not because I was pregnant!!). We met in the March and were engaged by June, we fully expected to wait until the following summer to marry, but the task of getting our dates to match, what with Ricky's work and my training dates set in stone things were not working out. We concluded that it would be best to get married in the December I loved the idea of a winter wedding, very romantic in my eyes. So, the next time we were up North, we had a date to go and visit the minister. Mum happened to be out, so I told dad "Ricky and I have changed the date to December for the wedding" and asked, "Is that ok?" He was very calm about it and said "yes, no problem just whatever you guys are happy with". Relieved I said "Great -we are off to see the minister". It was much later that I discovered my dad's laid-back approach was because he thought it was December the following year and not in four months' time! It was poor mum who broke the news to him after we were back in Aberdeen while she was discussing how close the wedding was!!

The next few months flew by, organising and arranging, me driving up and down the road deciding on bridesmaids' dresses, cake, flowers and all the usual stuff that came along with preparing for a wedding. During this time my dad was made redundant, and I remember being home for the weekend and the minister spoke to me after church (I still attended when I was home as after all these guys were family). He asked if I was still going ahead with the arranged date for the wedding as this would put a lot of financial pressure on my parents. I remember taking in what he was saying and feeling the weight of it hit me. My heart went into turmoil and I felt so guilty, I couldn't bear the thought of my parents struggling. Around this time, I received a letter from a concerned member of the church, outlining the verse of 'being unequally yoked', I was absolutely devastated and slightly angered that this person did not trust that I had considered this and had already brought this to God!!! My young heart really struggled to cope with the pressure I now felt for putting mum and dad in this position, and I now had the thought "was everyone taking about me marrying Ricky?" running through my mind. Thankfully I'd already had conversations about this with God, but mum picked up on the change in my mood and asked me "What's wrong?" I didn't want to lay the burden of what the minister had said on her so chose to show her the letter instead, we discussed it through, and she encouraged me. I knew mum had a strong relationship with God and she reminded me that when she first met Ricky, she knew he would be her son in law. So, the letter went in the bin. It was years later before I told Ricky about it as I didn't want to hurt him. In my heart I really struggled with why someone would do that, but I pushed these feelings down as I was getting married! This was supposed to be the most exciting time of my life!!The wedding plans all fell into place, Ricky's dad had given us money towards the wedding, so I was able to go get my wedding dress, and, in my eyes, this was helping my mum and dad out now I had been informed of the presumed position I was putting them in. In my heart, I felt my role was to try to save them from this pressure but looking back I wish I had spoken to them as this robbed my mum and me of the special experience of wedding dress shopping. God saw my heart and the pain in it, and I truly believe the way the rest of the wedding unfolded, that He was at the centre and in the detail of it all! We still talk about it to this day how every detail came together so smoothly, right down to the fact we didn't only have a piper, but a full pipe band. Family and friends travelled from all over on the 21st of December 1996. Ricky's friends and family even came down from Orkney, so I was to be introduced to the Orcadian ways!! With the two sets of friends and family coming together, two worlds collided, and it made for an amazing wedding. We have some hilarious stories to tell. Not only had we vowed in front of our friends and family but more importantly in front of God, to devote our selves to each other. God had seen our hearts, and nothing was hidden from him as we embarked on the adventure of our lives!

We spent our honeymoon in Aviemore and then up to Orkney for the New Year. This is where I first realised my now husband's love for this special place, he was so relaxed and talked freely about his love for his homeland.

Returning home, we settled back into life in Aberdeen. I moved into the one-bedroom flat Ricky owned and we set up home together. Ricky often tells the story of the time he went to work night shift, he came home to find that I had painted the whole living room!! Gone were the Elvis pictures and the black ash shelves, the football trophies were now in a box in the loft. The room was now lovely soft terracotta with throws on the sofa; he had just been introduced to my creative side!!!

Having been settled into married life for several months now, we had come to realise the expense of running a home as a couple and felt we needed more income, I started working for a nursing agency and doing the odd shift on my days off from training, so left us little time to do things as a couple. Now, Ricky was unhappy in his job, and we often spoke about his desire to move back to Orkney. I was also struggling, I was starting to feel overwhelmed what with being newly married, all the training and course work and now working extra shifts, it was all feeling way too much. I had the added pressure of my monthly cycle to contend with as I really struggled with pain and heavy bleeding. This was an issue growing up, and I remember passing out at school one day as the pain was so bad, my dad was phoned to come and get me. I just thought this was normal and some girls had it easier than others. I had missed some days at college due to this, so when I was called in to discuss with my lecturer regarding the amount off days off I'd had, I was now so overwhelmed I could not see the wood for the trees. I remember sitting with the lecturer discussing my progress and how well I was doing, but she was concerned about my days off and started explaining that things were going to get even more hectic and as my training came to an end the workload would increase and I really couldn't afford to fall behind. I explained to her about my issue with my monthly cycle, she suggested I should see the doctor and we arranged to meet the following week to see how I was doing, as by now I was crying and feeling extremely overwhelmed. Her suggestion of a visit to the doctor was not that simple. Because of an earlier experience in my teens which left me traumatised I had vowed never to go back to the doctor regarding this issue.

Going home to Ricky now extremely overwhelmed, my report of the meeting was not got good. I felt like a failure and thought I should leave nursing and put it down to the fact that I struggled academically, so what was the point, I was going to fail anyway. I recalled a conversation from a while back I had had with my mum about graduation. I remembered her words to me as she said, "One step at a time Jojo, don't get ahead of yourself". Now these words were comforting words from a mum who was keeping her daughter focused, but my heart felt that she didn't think I could do it. So, emotion backed up by words spoken, my heart decided I was leaving nursing as I was not going to be able to finish the course! My tutor was shocked when I tearfully told her I would be leaving nursing and as I thanked her for all her support. She was not convinced and told me that I had no reason academically to walk away; as I had passed everything so far and help would be available should I need it going forward. But the decision had been made in my heart; she could see my emotions and knew I was not for budging. She did however convince me to take six months out, that way the decision was not final, and I would have an opportunity in the future to return and pick up where I left off, so I agreed, but I already knew that wasn't what I would do. I was married now and anyway, it was my biology teacher who told me I had should be a nurse in the first place as it suited my personality. He was right, the caring nurturing side of me would have made a great nurse, but on the inside, it was not what I wanted. I was happily married now and saw Ricky as my knight in shining armour rescuing me, and so we decided to move to Orkney and start a new life. But the reality of it was, we were both unhappy with different aspects of our lives, so we opted for a new adventure across the sea!!

CHAPTER 5

The Orkney Days

Ricky applied for a job with British Airways at Kirkwall airport, and he was successful. We now could begin our plans to move. During this time, I fell pregnant; we were over the moon and really felt like life was falling into place. We decided to rent out our flat in Aberdeen. Ricky headed up to Orkney first as I waited behind to sort everything out and tie up all the loose ends. I would then head up to Tain, and Ricky came back down to spend the weekend with me and my parents before we headed back to Orkney to start our new life. I arrived at my God parents' house for the night as mum and dad were on holiday in Tenerife and were due back the following evening. Now, my morning sickness which was more of a coming in waves through the day kind of thing, it was hard to hide. I remember sitting in the kitchen feeling awful and my God mum looking me straight in the eye and asking, "What's wrong Jojo?" I burst into tears and told her as I just needed some help. She hugged me and the relief of saying I was pregnant out loud, just filled my heart with joy!! So, with that joy the two of us planned an exciting way to announce it to my mum and dad the following evening. It was mum and dads silver wedding anniversary that weekend also, so we planned the theme around that. I bought a silver box and put a little pair of baby's booties inside; this would be their anniversary gift. What better way was there to be told you're going to be grandparents!! I was grateful for the creative idea and we were both so excited for the next day when we could surprise them!!

As you can imagine this went down a treat and with lots of screaming and "I don't believe it" being shouted, tears of joy followed!! Ricky arrived the following day and we had a wonderful time celebrating the news. After a great weekend and with the car packed up, we said our goodbyes and left for our new life in Orkney.

The flat we were renting was not ready, so Ricky's best friend who lived with his parents (who owned the local butcher shop), were kind enough to let us live with them until the flat was ready. Their house was amazing, it looked out over the harbour and the town of Stromness, the view was breath-taking! I was extremely grateful to this family for taking us in and they made us feel so at home. I got myself booked in with the doctors and midwife; it was all becoming very real now, pregnancy and a new life living on this beautiful island. So why were my feelings on the inside not matching up? I put it down to pregnancy hormones!! My early stages of nausea still had not left and I remember the day I went into the kitchen to make some lunch, there was a big pot bubbling away on the cooker and I felt my stomach wrench, as I thought what is that smell!? As I lifted the lid the smell hit me full force and the sight of boiled ox tongue is what I was met with!! Lunch was now off the menu for me and I had to go and have a bath to recover!! This was the only downside of living with the butcher while pregnant. I learned this would be a weekly event, so I made myself scarce on that day. I found the days long when Ricky was at work and was always glad when he returned home. I really needed to find work and bring in some finance as we were starting to struggle. I headed to the local Job Centre in the hope of finding some work with a nursing agency, since I had experience working in the hospitals as a carer as well as the time I had spent at college I hoped I would get some relief hours, this would also be good not just financially but to help meet some new friends of my own. I had not bargained on the fact that being pregnant would be a stumbling block, but it clearly was, as employing someone in the caring profession, while pregnant is not the best idea as there are a lot of jobs you can't do. So why hire someone to do a job they can't do? This was a blow to my plan, so my mood dipped as I felt helpless and unable to contribute financially. I took this personally and really felt that I was letting Ricky down. Living with these friends that Ricky had known since childhood did not help my situation either. He had all these connections, and I heard all the stories and funny antics that they all got up to. Although I loved the relationship, they all had I, was starting to feel more and more insecure and isolated. Pregnancy hormones also played a part in this and while discussing this with Ricky, he just wanted his new wife to calm down (my dramatic flair upped its appearance whilst pregnant!!). "Once we get our own place it will get better" he said trying to reassure me and it worked as I managed to keep going.

The flat we were renting was now ready and it was time to get our stuff out of storage and move in! This was just fantastic and lifted my spirits greatly! Setting up our home together was just what I needed to make me feel at home on this beautiful island. Winter was drawing in and the days were dark and murky, we had a real coal fire in our living room, and this made the place so cosy and homely. Our flat was at the back of the butcher's shop, so it was a busy place to stay with lots of comings and goings. The main street was just out the front door, and I would head off down the street during the day and chat to people as I went. As it turned out everyone knew Ricky Bain so I was now known as "Ahhh you're Ricky Bains wife!!" This was all meant in a friendly manner but in my ever-increasing hormonal state and the huge hole in my own identity, it really got on my nerves!! Ricky reconnected with the Boys' Brigade leader and his wife, their home now became my new safe place. Their house was just as welcoming as Ricky had described it. Long hours spent round their table chatting and endless pots of tea, cakes from the local bakery and meals were all giving me a sense of home and family. They had two children and I was always delighted when asked if I could help with them. This family became a significant part of Ricky and my lives and to this day hold a very special place in our hearts. They invited us to go along to the neighbouring towns Baptist church, so we started going on a Sunday morning, it felt good in my heart, I embraced it and loved meeting new folks and enjoyed the teaching, but as always, I enjoyed the singing of the worship songs the best, my heart just soared! This became a way of life for us, heading off to church on a Sunday morning; it was also the place where I began to make some friends of my own. Ricky worked a lot of weekends so if he couldn't make it, I was happy to head off on my own to church. Around this time a lovely lady, the mother of Ricky's old Boy's Brigade leader, took me under her wing. Her husband was newly diagnosed with Alzheimer's so with my nursing background she asked me if I would look after him a couple of days a week, so she could head out and about and get things done. I was delighted to help, I did some chores around the house for her and helped in any way I could. It gave her peace of mind to know that he was not on his own. She also paid me for my time which was answered prayer as things had become financially very difficult on one wage and with a new baby to prepare for. I still missed home and my mum very much. I really struggled with her not being nearby. The worst times would be when I would watch the last boat leave at 3pm I would hear the horn blast and think "That's it. I am stuck here no way off this island now!!" Things got so bad one weekend, Ricky and I were fighting a lot, so I knew I needed to get away. I paid for a flight with my cheque book, even though I knew I had no money for it I knew that if I didn't go to see my family, my mum in particular, I would unravel!! The pressure of hormonal pregnancy was weighing down on me and I think even Ricky had had enough of my constant crying, so for both our sakes I went home for the weekend.

Mum and Dad collected me from Inverness airport, and we headed back to Tain, I was just delighted to be with them. Having a bath at home and just being looked after by them was wonderful. By the Saturday morning, my mum was very aware, that although this was a lovely visit it was however out of the blue and not with Ricky. So, I opened up a bit about how I was struggling in Orkney and being so cut off from everything I knew. I also confessed how we were struggling with finances as well as arguing a lot. We drank tea and chatted all morning and just got it all off my chest. It was a relief to discuss some of my feelings albeit, a bit jumbled. It was just so nice to spend time with my mum, and later she said, "Come on we are off to Inverness"!! So, we got ready quickly and headed away for a girls' day in town. She bought me some maternity clothes and we had lunch, we looked at baby clothes and discussed with excitement the new baby. It was just wonderful to be back in familiar settings and hanging out with mum. She sent me back to Orkney with a new sense of 'you can do this!!' She also handed me money to cover the plane ticket. As I flew back to the island, I had a fresh sense of 'everything is going to be ok'. Ricky and I settled back into life on the island, and with the winter now in full swing it was very bleak looking, the wind was wild, and the sharp cold would catch my breath, winters in Orkney are brutal! The end of the year was approaching and with attending church again, I started to think more about my faith and Jesus, as this time in my life was now like a big dipper rollercoaster! With all the pregnancy hormones, only being 21 and away from home, I can truly say it was the loneliest time of my life. As the end of the year came around, I remember sitting on New Year's Eve and feeling so lost. Ricky had gone out and I was sitting in the dark beside the fire. I cried out Jesus "I am not doing a very good job", and I remember thinking I needed to take off the boxing gloves as I felt I was fighting all the time. I said out loud "I surrender, you take charge I can't do this on my own anymore!" in my relief I cried softly, as the new year approached, I knew God was back in the driving seat.

Life took on more a of routine, I started helping another couple with their childcare as well as helping look after the elderly gentleman, so my day had purpose. During this time my brother came to the Island. He had split up with his long-term girlfriend, so he came to stay with us for some time out. It was great having him to stay. Late night chats, pots of tea and the sense of having family close made for a great visit. Although, I do remember one night my brother and Ricky headed out to the local pub for the karaoke night, I was not up for it so stayed at home by the fire. Now heavily pregnant, with all my insecurities about all the other females that Ricky seemed to know, I knew the idea of putting myself in that position was an evening that would not end well!! I felt tearful at the very thought of it, so me and my hormones stayed at home! I was happy for the boys to go and have some time out; I watched TV then went to bed. I remember waking up and thinking the house was really quiet, there was no sign of Ricky or my brother and it was nearly midnight, "they must still be out," I thought. I remember feeling overwhelmed with all sorts of emotions and flash backs from when I was younger, seeing my mum waiting for my dad to come home. These emotions filled my heart and along with my own insecurities, they left me feeling so upset and angry, I couldn't think straight! So, this caused me to think it would be a good idea to take myself off down the street to find out where they were. Still wearing my pyjamas, I threw on a jumper and headed out, desperately hoping I would bump into them before I reached the pub! You guessed it... I didn't!! Upon reaching the karaoke bar I scanned the room searching for my husband I spotted him having the time of his life laughing and joking surrounded by friends both male and female. When Ricky clocked me at the door he was met with a glare, I said nothing, turned around and left. I sobbed all the way home. When the boys eventually returned home, trying to convey what was going on on the inside of me did not go well. Ricky seemed oblivious to my pain, and a big argument between us followed with my brother chirping in, "It's not that big of a deal and you said it was fine for us to go out". They had no idea why I reacted so badly and frankly neither did I! I just knew I did not like feeling like this and I was letting them know!!

In the weeks that followed there was another incident that shook me, it was then I decided in my heart and told God "I cannot live on this island; it is not home for me." The father of the daughter I looked after tore into our home one day while Ricky was at work! He went on a rampage in our living room shouting like a crazy man, he scared the life out of me! When he finally left, I fled to my safe place, the home of the lovely couple on the main street. I was hysterically crying, they looked after me and listened to what had happened. Ricky found me there later that evening when he came home from work. I think it was then that Ricky knew the life we had hoped for in Orkney was not panning out as we had planned.

With the birth of our first baby now fast approaching, the overwhelming sense that 'I cannot live on this island' had not left me. Ricky and I chatted many times over the weeks that followed; he finally said, "if you really don't like it here, I will look for a job back in Aberdeen". I felt such relief and it helped me cope with the remainder of my pregnancy, I thought "I can do this if it's not forever". Spring was arriving in full bloom, and the island was starting to come alive.

Katie was born on the 13th of May 1998; my mum had made it up on time and she was allowed into the delivery room. The doctor and the midwife were there along with Ricky and mum. Having been a student nurse in the past, any time a student asked to be in the room I always said yes, so she was there too!!!This made for a busy labour ward! Katie arrived to the soundtrack from the Titanic film and a room full of people!! It brings a smile to my face to think that to this day Katie still thrives in a room full of people. She is a social butterfly!!

I was overjoyed and could not believe I'd done it after 26 hours of hard labour, Katie was back to back and I now know that this is one of the most painful deliveries. I remember sitting in bed after everyone had left, just looking at this tiny bundle, I just couldn't believe she was mine!! I thought my heart was going to explode with love!! I finally knew what I always wanted to be... A MUM!! It was such a joy, I loved every minute of it and the midwife at Kirkwall hospital was amazing. I had never thought much about breast feeding but she spent time with me, and I will be forever grateful to her as it set me up on a pathway for the way ahead, and the expense that was saved in not having to buy milk was awesome!!

Taking Katie home from hospital was the best feeling as I could not wait to enjoy time with her and begin life as a family. I embraced it, all the late-night feeds, bathing, pacing the floor, the lot!! It was just such a privilege. I remember the health visitor coming past and she said to me "enjoy every minute, even if you go on and have more children you will never get this time back with Katie". This was good advice, even when I did go on to have more children; I still made time when it was just me and the baby. Being a mum is a privilege not to be taken lightly and later when I expand on this area of my life and the roller-coaster of raising five children you will see the sense of 'what a privilege' never ever left me.

When Katie was a couple of weeks old, we headed down to Aberdeen to introduce her to our family and friends. It was a weird feeling travelling with a newborn, but we embraced it, it was also great to get off the island and show her off. During this time Ricky, true to his promise, went to an agency and signed up for some work. He even he got an interview at an oil company while we were there, and he heard the next day that he had got the job! I was just over the moon and so thankful my prayers were answered!! We could now finally make plans to head back down to Aberdeen. Looking back, I will always be grateful to my wise husband who made the selfless choice to save his marriage and family by making the decision to return to Aberdeen. Anyone who knows Ricky knows he is an Orkney lad at heart and always will be! Orkney still holds a special place in our hearts, I do love going back to visit, as some of our favourite people to hang out with still live there. Katie loves the fact she is the only true Orcadian in the family as Ricky only moved up there with his parents when he was a year old. Before we left, I remember the pastor of the church praying for us, he said "the first week you arrive back in Aberdeen find a good church and make yourself a home there, it is vital, and don't think you will do it later as later never comes" I left with this advice ringing in my ears, along with his suggestion as to which church to go due to its Orkney connections. This was top of the list for when we would arrive back. Closing the door to this chapter in our lives, we set off back to the flat we had first started our married life in but now as a family.

CHAPTER 6

FAMILY

We made it back, all our belongings were shipped over, and Saturday was spent setting up the flat and getting beds made! Mum was down helping us get settled and helping with Katie. After a busy day, we were shattered! It would have been easy to think 'we'll look at finding that church next week', but with the words of the pastor ringing in my ears, there was something on the inside of me that knew there was truth in what he said. Ricky went for a drive to see if he could find the church he had mentioned so we would know where to go in the morning, but as the church at this point was held in a school there were no signs indicating that this was where the church was held, so he came back unsure if that was it. Undeterred we got up the next day and headed to church and were relieved to see the sign confirming we were in the right place. Church in a school was a new concept for me and was excited to experience it. Unbeknown to us at the time, these people would become our family. We received such a warm welcome, and true to the reviews we got before attending, this was a church with a very strong Orkney connection. So, for Ricky this was definitely a selling point and for me with the band and the worship songs that hit my heart so powerfully I knew we would fit in there. Over the next few weeks, we made some friends and were invited to what they called a fellowship meal. The whole church was there celebrating an anniversary of when the church had first started. It was great to get out and not have to cook! Katie was in her element as a baby being passed around and adored by all these lovely women. We felt very at home and relaxed with these people, they were about to be introduced to the dynamic of Ricky and my relationship. This story has been told many times since by our friends who were at the table at the time, and thankfully we can laugh, as this was the start of a lifelong friendship, a true gift from God! Katie was just starting to find her feet at this time, and she was padding back and fore on top of the table going between Ricky and I, with a cheeky glint in his eye Ricky said "oh that's how I met her mother, tabletop dancing!!! "I was horrified!! The nerves on the inside of me were doing somersaults as I tripped over my words trying to explain my husband's sense of humour, but they were all laughing and had caught on to it. This about sums Ricky and I up at that stage in our lives, I so want to fit in, and he is just free being himself in any environment. We soon became aware that our story of meeting in a nightclub was also not your traditional way in church for meeting someone, as it is usually one of the first questions when getting to know other couples, they ask "oh how did you meet?" It was also not really the done thing for young Christian girls to be out in the night clubs, so I adopted the phrase, "oh I was back-slidden" and this seemed to be acceptable, or so I thought. But looking back at my time I never stopped praying or conversing with God, the heart Jesus caught at 13 was still very much full of his love, it was the church I had fallen out of love with.

Over the coming months Ricky went on a bit of a journey with finally opening his heart up to the fact that Jesus had died on the cross for him. I remember after one service as Ricky turned to speak to one of the men in the church, he came straight out with "so Ricky how's your heart before God?", this was a statement that really challenged him and sent him on a journey of asking the question to God himself. Ricky came to his own conclusion that he was doing all the right things by going to church..... God was more interested in his heart. This was the point in his journey that he finally opened his heart and as his wife I was delighted. Not long after this we made the decision to have Katie dedicated. It was different to what I was used to, as I had grown up with the concept of baby christening, was seen as your baptism so no need to do it when you're older. This was more of a dedicating your baby to God until they can make their own choice which to me, made sense.

Life back in Aberdeen was going great, it felt good to reconnect with friends and make new ones. But Life was about to get a whole lot more interesting! I started to feel unwell, Katie was six months old and I thought "this feels very familiar" and sure enough a test confirmed I was pregnant!! We were shocked but overjoyed. Mum came down a few weekends later and as she was playing with Katie, I said "tell Granny you are going to be a big sister!" Mum was really excited although she did say "how are you going to manage?" Although deep down I shared the same concerns, and felt the weight of what lay ahead, my choice was to push into the truth of what I already knew. No matter how hard the next season was going to be, the love in my heart and the joy of being a mum would be the thing that would set me up for the challenges that lay ahead. I felt like the luckiest woman alive to be pregnant again so soon, I remember praying and asking God for this next baby and Katie to be best friends regardless of what sex the baby was. I spoke to Katie all the time about the baby in my tummy and what an amazing big sister she was going to be.

Soon after finding out I was pregnant, Ricky and I had been chatting about getting baptised as we both agreed it was important to us and the church we attended was a Baptist church, so there was lots of teaching around it. It felt like the next step in our journey of faith together. So, we made plans and arranged to be baptised. Mum came down for the service along with Ricky's Boys Brigade leader. It was such a day of celebration and being pregnant at the same time felt special.

Over the coming weeks and months, it was all systems go. We needed to put the flat on the market and try to find a house now our family was growing in number. It was such an exciting time and we ended up moving not too far from where we were which was great seeing as we liked the area. I remember sitting at the bottom of the stairs in our new home waiting for the truck to arrive with all our belongings and feeling so happy, I just couldn't believe this was our home. It was an end terrace house with two bedrooms and a garden, but it felt like a palace to me. With all this new space we loved having people over, so our home became an open house where the kettle was always on the boil. To this day this is still how we operate as a family.

During my pregnancy, we had a family tragedy. When Ricky was around 24 years old, his mum sadly passed away, this left his dad to care for his older brother Robbie who had learning difficulties. Now getting much older, his dad along with social workers decided that his brother should try living independently of him with the help of assisted living. Robbie had been in the housing for a couple of months when Ricky received a phone call at work one Saturday morning to say that he had been out all night and had not returned home. Ricky came home early explained what had happened and left to look for him. With no success he came back home where he received a phone call from his dad who had been informed that a body had been pulled out of the water that morning , the captain of the Orkney boat that was coming into harbour had spotted the body and alerted the coast guard. All this information was coming at me as Ricky headed off to be with his dad and wait for the police to arrive. I phoned my parents to speak to them but could not get hold of them, so I phoned my God parents. It was my God dad that answered the phone, but as I opened my mouth to speak no words came out, just hysterical screaming!! I completely lost it!! I heard his voice but could not rein in my emotions, eventually he was shouting down the phone very angrily at me. The sound of his voice shouting "Joanne," was enough to snap me back into some sort of rational thought process. I was then able to tell him what was going on, he said he would go and find my mum and dad. I knew now that my role was to be there for Ricky and Katie, this was his brother and I needed to focus on that to be able to function. Mum and dad arrived down, my dad went with Ricky to identify the body as his own father was emotionally unable to do it, he was completely broken. This was a season where Ricky and I learnt to completely lean on God, as if left to us we would have gone under. I saw in Ricky over the coming days and weeks, a strength that I had never seen before. Now he was a physically strong man, but this was a different kind of strength, and he will testify that it was a defining moment in his walk with God. As we walked out the grief and trauma of this event, 'God is our strength when we are weak,' is definitely how we would both describe the way we navigated this time. He comforts the broken hearted, I watched this happen in my husband's life, and with the prayers and love of the family and friends around us we walked out this season.......

It was now summer, and we were preparing for the arrival of our new baby, the last few weeks of pregnancy were long and hard going with Katie still being a baby herself, she was only 14 months old. Thankfully though, she was very independent, from a young age she wanted to walk everywhere, which really helped. We would go for walks after Ricky got home from work, one, to try and get my labour going as I was now overdue, and two, to tire Katie out so she would sleep all night!! I was now eight days overdue, during a visit to see my midwife she said to me," oh you could go anytime, you won't see the weekend out "I was so excited and relieved. I phoned mum and she came down ready to watch Katie, the weekend passed and still no baby! I remember phoning my midwife on the Monday morning; she said to me "please tell me you've had your baby" "no still hanging on!!" I sighed, "Put the phone down" she said, "and I will call you back." Within a few minutes she was back on the phone telling me to get down to the hospital as they were expecting me, she was so apologetic and said "I was so sure you would go over the weekend I am sorry I should have booked you in sooner." I was just happy that today was the day we were going to meet the newest member of the Bain family. At 18.45 Hannah slipped into our world. The love that filled my heart the moment I set eyes on Hannah was overwhelming, as being Katies mum was more than I had ever hoped or imagined. I think every parent's worry when they have more children is; what's it going to be like sharing the love they have with more than one child. But the love that hit my heart in that instant was so overpowering I realised it's not a case of having to share the love around but the moment the baby is born you receive a whole new pot of love just for that child. I just couldn't take my eyes off her, looking at this new member of our family and thinking, "wow someone so different and yet very familiar all at the same time." I was now realising the best meal in the whole world was the tea and toast after giving birth. I remember after having Katie, saying "this is the best thing I have ever tasted." I now had that same thought, as I gazed at Ricky holding Hannah and eating the buttered toast and sipping on my hot tea. We phoned mum and shared the news that she was a granny again, and we could not wait to come home to introduce her and to give Katie a hug as, I missed her so much.

In those early days another couple came along side us, and the husband was key in Ricky's understanding of the bible. They met weekly and as Ricky asked questions he grew in his knowledge and understanding. We were well looked after and were invited to dinner at their house. I remember walking into their beautiful home and thinking wow!! Everything was immaculate I could feel the sting of some old insecurities in my heart starting to resurface, ones I had formed from a young age they were chasing down my thoughts. I pushed them back and told her "what a beautiful home you have", and I meant it. We had a lovely evening with delicious food and lots of chat, I loved listening to their story of how they had met and found God, and it was a fascinating journey they had been on. During conversation it was pointed out to me that they had a pure wool carpet, and nothing had ever been spilt on it!! I was now nervous as Ricky was always spilling; he was messier than the kids! One evening in the weeks that followed we had finished our meal and were relaxing in the living room. And true to form as Ricky was chatting and telling a story, his foot slipped and yes, knocked over his glass of red wine!! I felt sick to my stomach, they were so lovely about it, but I was devastated and had a right go at Ricky later. An accident like this is really just something that a lot of people would brush off, but I'd chew it over churning up my insides and over think it so much. Insecurities were nipping at my heels, with having two small children and not a lot of sleep; this resulted in even more unhealthy thought patterns. I would make comparisons and not always come to the healthiest of conclusions. I would often be invited to their home for a coffee date, something I was still getting used to, as being a highland girl coffee dates were not a thing, it was always 'just pop in any time for a cuppa the kettle is always on!!' I remember one occasion when Katie was playing with their daughter, and I heard this scream! Katie had bitten her! I was horrified, both girls were crying as I tried to calm things down. I got Katie to apologise but the little girl was screaming. Her mum was equally stressed and reacting to the screaming, at this point I was finding it all so overwhelming I said, "we'd better leave", and so I drove home crying. When trying to relay all this to Ricky at the dinner table and voicing it out loud it didn't seem so bad after all. He felt I had handled it well, giving Katie a row and explaining biting is bad and getting her to apologise. But, on the inside, it was still going over and over in my mind, and over thinking was definitely an issue for me! That horrible feeling in the pit of your stomach, feelings of 'this is my fault,' reinforced by the other mum's reaction to the situation, she must have thought it was my fault too.

Church life was keeping us busy; this definitely was a family church and doing life together outside a Sunday service was part of their lifestyle. Everyone was put into what was called care groups and we had the loveliest older couple as our leaders, these groups were held in homes and as we had a young family, we offered our home to be used, it meant Ricky and I could both attend. As a young couple journeying in faith these nights became a valuable key in our learning. We were taught and loved by this very mixed group of people, and as always, for me the sound of the voices singing in our home along with the guitar was very special, the sense of God's presence was tangible. I loved opening our home up and we always had a steady flow of friends and family over for dinner or to stay for the weekend. Ricky would have some of the boys over to watch the football, and I would often have the girls over watching films and enjoying time out while the children were in bed.

Over the next couple of years life settled into a routine. I had started to help run the crèche at church which I loved and because the church was held at a school at that time, we had to arrive early to set up as everything was in storage and had to be taken out. So, Sundays were a busy day, we would be at the church for 8.30am, Ricky would help with the seats, banners and any heavy lifting as I would be setting up crèche and preparing snacks for the children. It would all need taking down again after the service, so it was a long morning. Most weeks after church we'd have folks back for food, or we would be invited to go to someone else's home. We became family to each other, and it was just fab. As a church we also did summer family picnics at the end of term, they were always very competitive especially when it came to the fathers' races, we would often invite our friends who weren't church goers to come along as these were so much fun. The highlight in church for me was still always the worship and the band, when I would be setting up the crèche, I'd listen to the band rehearse and think how amazing it would be to be part of that team. I would sing along, and just like in my early church days, if a song hit my heart, I'd think "oh we are in for a good service today, great song choice!!" Music for me remains my favourite way to communicate with God, whatever my emotion I can connect to the heart of who He is to me through my worship, along with my journaling, and leaving my concerns or over thinking, firmly with Him. My heart has always been sold out for who Jesus is and the love in my heart is worn on my sleeve for all to see, and as God is all seeing anyway so there is no hiding from Him.

Living on the outskirts of the city was great, the girls were now attending nursery and it was a fantastic wee place, the staff were so friendly. The girls were so happy I was making good friends, one of which like me, was more of a 'kettle is always on kind of girl', this made life so much easier. We became great friends and were at each other's houses most days. I fell pregnant with our third child in the year 2000 it was just the best news. This time round we decided to find out the sex of the baby, something we had not done with the others, and it was the only time we did find out. The radiographer said to me "congratulations you have a hat-trick", funny she used football talk when telling me!! So, another girl was to join our tribe, we called her Rebecca and spoke to her by name the whole pregnancy. I was pregnant over the summer months, it was a hot year and I lived on ice-lollies!! One morning Ricky was just heading off to work, as I was hanging out the washing, we had a split level garden and to get to the washing line there were two sets of steps with four or five steps on each, as I turned to come back inside I fell down both sets of steps and landed on my bump!! I was around seven and a half months pregnant, and my bump was quite big. Ricky came rushing out, even with my knee was burst open, and my only thought was for the baby!! Ricky got hold of a friend to take Katie and Hannah as he took me to hospital. We arrived at A&E and they took me straight through to be seen, my leg was in agony and I could hardly walk. The whole time I was praying and asking God to please take care of my baby. When we finally got seen by the doctor, she wanted to stich my knee first, but I was begging her to listen to Rebecca's heartbeat, she assured me that once I was stitched up I would be transferred to the maternity ward to be monitored. My mum made her way down from Tain to look after the girls and I spent a night in hospital being monitored. All was well, and Rebecca seemed un-phased by the eventful morning, we even managed to get a scan of her albeit the back of her head. What a scare we all got, I was very sore for a few weeks afterwards. I was relieved and very thankful to only have a knee injury. Church family and friends rallied and helped get the girls back and fore to nursery while I was struggling to walk.

I was now overdue; this was not unexpected as it was the same with my other two pregnancies, so it was business as usual. I had just dropped a friend and her daughter off at their house after being out on a play date, I was driving home when a car appeared from nowhere, driving at top speed! I thought "this car is going to hit me!!" Sure enough, it went head on into the front of my car!! It then started reversing and the whole of its front was hanging off, sparks were flying, I couldn't believe what was happening and I couldn't think straight!! The car disappeared around the corner, and with the noise this created people were now coming out of their houses to see what was going on. I started to shake and Katie and Hannah were crying so I got out and went to the back seat to comfort them. People began asking if I was ok, but as I tried to remain calm for the girls crowds heightened response and cries of "I can't believe what's just happened" was all too much, my emotions took over and I began to cry. One of the ladies saw I was pregnant and phoned for an ambulance and the police to come. My friend who lived just round the corner, heard the commotion and was now on the scene, she looked after the girls and got in touch with Ricky. I was now on my way to hospital for another overnight stay and a night of monitoring more scans!! But Rebecca seemed quite happy in there and in no hurry to come out!!

It was around this time I started to understand how to deal with fear and how to bring it to God, as there had been two traumatic experiences while pregnant and I could feel things on the inside of me getting all in a spin!! I remember feeling the fear that something bad was going to happen but through journaling and prayer along with the verses in the bible that talk about God knowing us before he formed us in the womb. I would speak to God and thank Him for knowing Rebecca and that He holds the future, and so I would leave my concerns with Him. In life we are not promised an easy road and it's full of tough situations we must face, but in these moments, we have a choice; to let fear overwhelm us or to push into the faith of who God is. I know my choice will always be Him.

Three days later I was sitting in the hairdresser's, I thought I would treat myself after the last couple of months I'd had and before life got busier with being a mum to three girls. I was laughing and joking with the hairdresser, she was concerned because I was over my due date and did not want a baby born in her shop!! I assured her that I was always late and not to worry. The radio was on in the salon, the place fell silent as we listened to the news that was coming from America. Two aeroplanes had just flown into the twin towers in New York, no one could believe it!! I finished up at the hairdressers and rushed home to Ricky who was watching the girls. He had the news on the TV; it was horrifying to watch as we sat silently praying as the events unfolded on the screen. A national tragedy that left the world forever changed.

Three days later on the 14th of September 2001, Rebecca finally decided she would make an appearance. Once things got going, she was wasting no time and within 25 minutes of going into the labour ward she was born!! My whole body was shaking with the shock of how quick it was!! Rebecca was finally here, she arrived in the morning and after all my checks we were allowed home and by evening I was cosy on the sofa with all my girls and just so grateful Rebecca was here and she was safe. I did think to myself "I wonder what plans you have for her Lord as that was some pregnancy and a real battle to bring her into the world!!" So, as I look today at the amazing young woman she has become and Knowing Gods determination to bring her into the world, I've become her biggest cheerleader as she chases after the plan He has for her life.

CHAPTER 7

FULL STEAM AHEAD

I was now mum to three girls, what an adventure!!! Katie was three, Hannah was two, and now with Rebecca as a new-born, life was full!! With it being an eventful summer, we had not done anything fun with the girls, so we decided while Ricky had the time off now Rebecca was here, it was time to take a trip. We realised with three small children a day trip would be enough! The girls wanted to go to the zoo, so off we went to Edinburgh for the day. I had a visit from the midwife the day before and I had a bad case of mastitis, which she had already prescribed antibiotics for, so she asked, "are you sure a trip to Edinburgh is wise?" I assured her I would be fine and that I would get a sleep in the car as it's a three-hour drive, and this to a sleep deprived mum is 'pure bliss'!! I really wanted to do something fun for Katie and Hannah as the lead up to Rebecca's birth had been such an intense time, so a fun family trip was exactly what our family needed!! It was a great day out and yes, I needed regular painkillers to deal with my rising temperature and flu like symptoms due to the mastitis, but it was so worth it to see the girls running around having fun. We had a full day out and later went to my brothers who lived nearby. We bathed the kids, put them in their pyjamas and headed up the road; I slept all the way home!

I was so happy to be a mum, I saw many of the obstacles as a challenge and learnt to think on my feet as we moved and grew as a family of five. This was also true on the days I felt so exhausted, and sleep deprived, when I would forget what a privilege it is to be a mum. I remember one day sitting on the bottom of our stairs and feeling so overwhelmed as both girls were going to nursery, one in the morning session and one in the afternoon, there was a lot of going back and forth. Rebecca was almost a year old at this point. I put my head in my hands and thought "I can't do this", the still small voice on the inside replied "yes you can," I looked up at the wee faces looking into my eyes to see if all was well, I wiped my tears, scooped them up and said "come on girls let's get to nursery!!" This is what it looks like when we read in the scriptures that He is strong when we are weak. I chose that day to push past the urge to go back to bed and pull the duvet over my head; instead I pushed into that still small voice and echoed it in my heart "I can do this!!"

It's the little decisions we make that are important as we navigate our way through the day-to-day. The days I would lose it with tiredness, I would hug the girls and say "sorry mummy is tired", or the days I would choose to put them first and they had no idea of the cost, the days of tough love because boundaries are important, the days of counting to three but having no idea what happens when you get to three!! The constant returning the toddler to the step when time out takes longer trying to get them to sit, than the actual time that you wanted to have them in time out for! Constant love on all levels, because I love you is not just a word, it is displayed in so many ways throughout a day when raising children. There were also the self-care days, when being in your pjs all day watching movies, or letting the kids pull out every toy in the house as I soaked in the bath just to get some time out! All of this including the bedtime stories and nightly prayers were foundations that looking back have become, the deep roots in the young adults I look at today.

The trek back and forth to nursery took a good half hour, with the girls walking and me pushing a buggy, I was very fit and so were the girls. With Katie in morning nursery and Hannah in the afternoon class, I remember one day we were all tired and I was saying come on girls we are going to be late; Hannah looked me straight in the eye and said "I hate you mummy!!" I remember being shocked as it stung my heart, but out of my mouth came "that's ok I love you!! "She started crying saying "I didn't mean it I didn't mean it", my beautiful wee red headed girl was expressing her tiredness and then instantly felt guilty.

In the evenings when Ricky would return home from work and dinner would be cleared away, we would have what we called the mad hour before bath time! Ricky would often put music on, and the kids would dance about. I remember thinking in my heart how special these times were, I would also have a sense of how special our kids were I would say this to Ricky many times "Ricky there is something special about our children," he would laugh and tell me," all parents say that about their kids".

Church life was still just as busy, I was going along to a ladies' bible study called Babies Invited Bible Study, BIBS for short. This would be a place of learning and growing in my knowledge of the bible, as well as getting time out as they had a crèche for the children. It was originally held at this older couple's home the atmosphere was welcoming and friendly. They had the living room set up as the crèche and a smaller room where we went to have our study. With plenty delicious cakes and coffee on offer this was a great way to kick off the weekend as it was held on a Friday morning. During one study we were talking about miracles, the question was asked "what is a miracle to you?" I had written 'children', this sparked a conversation, as many had not thought children were a miracle, they were thinking along the lines of people being healed. I was asked why I had written 'children', I explained about the women I knew who could not have children; I had seen the pain this caused as they walked their journey out. I never take for granted that children are little miracles' when you think about how they are made and formed, what the body goes through, and God knows each one of them!! It also fuels my conversations with God around why some are born with differences and illness; it causes me pain in my heart when I think about it. Being a swimming teacher now and helping many children on a one-to-one basis who face many challenges, my life is richer for them being in the world, they are some of the most amazing children with equally amazing parents. It's a joy to be part of their journey, even just a small part. When we just hang around in the bitterness of why this has had to happen, we get lost in our hearts, but if we lift our eyes trusting in God we can be over-comers, knowing that if we feel the pain of it, what he feels is even greater. We are a family that has faced many tragedies, how we navigate through pain and grief is down to our faith in what Jesus has done for us and the relationship we have with him, as his love catches our hearts when we are in pain and our minds are filled with questions.

We were rapidly out growing our family home, we now had five of us in a two-bed roomed house, the girls' room had two sets of bunk beds in it. We were also struggling financially; I had returned to work doing night settling to bring in extra money. Our finances were messy, and this overwhelmed me, I could not see the wood for the trees. At times I felt like a total failure, and that I had let God down, as I was not managing this part of my life well. It didn't help when money was preached about in church, it added to the failure feeling! I had many conversations with God about this; I cried and kept asking for forgiveness, for failing him in this area. I remember the day he spoke to me about this and as I was reading in my bible about King David, I suddenly had a light bulb moment. When David was a young boy God used him to take down a giant with just one stone. No one looked at him and saw anything special even his own family didn't think much of him; he was the boy who took them lunch and tended the sheep. He also went on to have an affair and kill a man! But David is known in the bible as a man after God's heart. Through this story I now understood the concept of God's grace. We are human after all and despite our mistakes and wrong choices God still loves us and wants the best for us. In that moment I felt a wave of love take the feeling of failure and replace it with the peace and love I know came from God himself. Yet again I realigned my heart with the promise I read all those years ago as a 13-year-old.' I know the plans I have for you declares the Lord, plans to prosper you and not to harm you!! '

I now had to walk this out as I couldn't stay sitting in my seat, we had a home that needed to be sold, finances to sort out and a new home to find. I was still working for the nursing agency, and I had to have my time sheets in on a certain day for them to be processed and paid into my bank. Life was busy and one week I missed the deadline! I was crying telling Ricky, as I knew we needed that money to survive that week. We had a big fight and looking back I see it was Ricky's fear, but he was so angry at me for forgetting my time sheets. I told him "don't worry I have prayed about it and God knows", he laughed and said, "what's God going to do about it!!" I stormed out of the room, as I walked past the front door, I saw an envelope sitting on the mat, and my heart raced as I knew God had answered my prayer! I picked up the envelope and opened it, sure enough, the exact amount that I would have been paid was in this envelope. I came back into the living room with mixed emotions crying, laughing and still annoyed at Ricky for our fight, and said triumphantly "this is what God has done about it!!!" This was the first time in our lives we had seen a miracle in our finances, we could write a whole book about many others, but this was to mark the start of a journey we would go on with God around finances. It also became the launch pad in the way we trusted and believed God for the next steps in our journey with him.

Our very good friends had moved out to the country and were living on an estate that owned many houses and the rent was reasonable. We chatted through with them how would we go about applying for a house, with both Ricky and I coming from smaller communities, we were both drawn to the country way of living. We had many people praying for us at this time and after many phone calls we managed to secure a house in the village of Dunecht. Our house sold, and our friends rallied, as we moved out to the large three-bedroom two living room house in the country. We enrolled the children in school, Katie in p2 and Hannah would start her school journey here in p1, Rebecca started playgroup. This was such a happy season in our lives; we embraced the way of life out there with vast green areas for the children letting off steam. When Ricky would come home from work, we would cross the road and head into the spacious estate, it was like a fairy tale for the girls with a castle to walk round. We all have such great memories of these times and today it's still a favourite place to go walking.

We were still very much involved in church life. With the ever-growing sense of family that we had with them all, our new home became a place where we loved to have everyone over for lunch or dinner, the children loved it as well! I was still running the crèche and with the church having now moved into its own building life was exciting and the church was growing fast. Around this time the worship team were looking for new members and my heart desperately wanted to be involved. I remember praying about this but with my lack of self-worth and the nagging voice in my head saying, "you can't even sing!!" I put it to the back of my mind. But one Sunday a friend of mine said to me they had had a dream about me being involved in the worship team and asked was it something I would be interested in! I was so amazed, as God had seen my heart and answered my prayer through a trusted friend who was a worship leader at the time, and they asked me along to the worship team meeting. I was like an excited child, the thought that God had seen my heart and made a way, and the fact that I had been asked along was all very over whelming, and when I get excited, I talk a lot!!! This did not put anyone off at the team get together and was later invited to an audition! I felt sick to my stomach and the nerves had me in tears, Ricky tried to reassure me saying "you don't have to do it no one is making you!!" But he didn't understand how important this was to me, and I could not put it into words. I found the courage to go along and meet with the worship leaders; there were a couple of others that were looking to join so at least I was not on my own. I was asked questions that were easy enough to answer as it was all about my faith and relationship with Jesus, this was easy for me to talk about, then they said "let's go and see what you sound like with a microphone", my heart was pounding in my chest as I had no idea of how it sounded! I prayed in tongues the whole time in my head, speaking to God and asking him to make me sound ok. When it was my turn for the microphone, I opened my mouth to sing and as the words came out, I felt the physical touch of the Holy Spirit. This was the first time I experienced a tremble on my top lip and to this day as I worship this still happens; I call it my 'Elvis lip'. No one would ever know, but I do, and as I open my mouth to bring praise to the one whom on the inside of me is my all in all, this brings me confidence. This is the part of my walk with Him that no one sees, but when I sing the connection is so powerful it blows me away. People have said to me over the years "you have such an anointing for worship", I had no idea what that meant at the time, but I now know it's where the truth of who I am and my relationship with my Jesus, my grateful heart to God and my thankfulness to the Holy Spirit gets to shine. My insecurities were all still there but I would have to tuck them all away to have the courage to get on the stage, my eyes were drawn to the window at the back of the church, as I looked out at the clouds in the sky I'd focus on them and not the congregation. In the early days this is how I overcame my nerves, my insecurities and the self-doubt, and over the years this would be a whole other journey God would take me on as he developed me from the inside out.

My ever-growing struggle with the divide between the church and the world would battle on on the inside of me. I remember God giving me a picture of steppingstones, and in my usual questioning way I went on a bit of a journey to discover what He meant. I saw it as, not everyone understands church life or the need for God, and so they would never come to a church building. Because I was around mums and small children as this was the stage of life I was at, I went to the church leaders and asked if I could I start a toddler group. The vision was, that this would be a safe place for the mums of the community to come along to the building and get to know the people on the inside breaking down the preconceived ideas of what church was. I saw this as the first steppingstone. A couple of mums with the same heart got together, and we made ourselves available on a Monday morning. Over the first few months no one other than church mums came, this was disappointing, as this was not the vision! We asked the church prayer team to pray along with us for the community mums to start coming along, as if this continued I would stop running it, as we did not need more dates for church folk to meet, we had plenty of them! I remember reaching out to the local health visitors letting them know of our group, we invited them along to visit the building and to introduce ourselves. Over the next few weeks, we started to get referrals and the group burst into life, Little Fishes was birthed. There are so many stories that have come out of this group, but to this day I will be forever grateful to God for the vision of the steppingstones. One of my very good friends now tells the story of being a young mum living in this area and coming along to the group. She wanted to help her son mix with other children and to socialise herself, but I remember her words clearly, "I will have nothing to do with the God thing!!" She is now mum to four children and along with her husband she started on her own journey of faith. I had the privilege of holding her towel at her baptism; we are great friends today and have weathered the highs and lows of this journey in life. I no longer run this group; I passed on the baton and now almost 15 years later it is still running and has an impact in the local community today.

CHAPTER 8

THE SCHOOL GATES

Over my 23 years of being a mum, I have stood at the school gates countless times, and over my parenting journey, at four different primary schools. If leaving your children at school for the first time does not bring you to tears, in my experience, the school gates definitely will!! When Katie started primary one, I remember the emotions being so overwhelming. It caught my breath and opened up an emotional insecurity in me that I had not felt since my own school days, only now I was the adult having to navigate my way around other parents' thoughts and opinions. Thankfully Katie was so ready for it and skipped into school, many of her friends form nursery were going to the same school, and so she was confident going in, this definitely helped. One day I was standing chatting with some of the mums who had been talking about their children getting the tin of words home and how exciting it was. I realised that Katie hadn't been given hers yet, so on the inside I went straight to my default of 'what am I doing wrong?' I had a chat with Katie about it, she didn't seem fazed about not having her tin of words, but this now became a big discussion point at the dinner table with Ricky of what could be wrong? Ricky suggested I speak to the teacher as she always brought the children out and was happy to chat to parents. The teacher was lovely and told me some of the other teachers did it differently and handed out the children's word tins all at the same time, but she herself likes to wait until the child shows an interest in reading words. She felt Katie was definitely starting to show interest and I was not to panic, as in the next few weeks she would get the words home. But listening to the chat around the playground there were lots of opinions flying around about the styles of teaching and who thought what, I started to feel overwhelmed as I wanted to take the advice of the teacher but when standing about chatting to the mums before the kids came out, it always left me feeling awful on the inside, it was a turmoil I did not like, and was constantly checking my judgment of the situation. Along with my own struggles I had in school fuelled by the conversations some of the mums were having, I was struggling to see it for what it was. I had a discussion with the pastor's wife from the church as she was a teacher and I wanted to hear her thoughts on it, she settled my fears and confirmed what the teacher had said and explained that all children learn at different paces and it's not something you can measure at that age, she went on to say "when you're a young adult no one remembers when they got their tin of words home or what stage they started reading at, only that they can read and they either enjoy it or not". Wise words and I knew it to be true!! I told her how standing at the school gates made me feel, she encouraged me to be myself and not to be swayed by others' opinions and that I was doing a great job with the girls, and I was a good mum. These words were like honey to the soul, someone saying you are doing a good job makes all the difference. I'm not sure what it was about the mix of mums at the school gates that sent me into such a spin but there were times I would pray in my head all the way to school to settle my thoughts, but other times I would walk along with some of the other mums and have a great time chatting with them all.

With Katie's first year of school coming to an end, I now had my first year of standing at the school gates under my belt and it was now time to leave the city and head to our new home in the country. The country school definitely had a different vibe. Our new neighbours had a child starting primary one at the same time as Hannah. This was just amazing, and I really felt like this was a gift from God to me as I was so nervous, but over the summer we had become friends and so the school gates did not feel so daunting. Looking back over the years I can definitely see that it was my own insecurities that had me reacting in the ways I did when it came to the school gates. But over the years with my faith and prayer life helped navigate my way around them. As the children were growing up, they would be more aware of my reactions so I would need to keep them in check as I certainly did not want to pass any of this on to them. As the years went on the school grew due to the village expanding, so Hannah was put into a split class and she was in the lower age group of the mix. We were told by way of a letter that was handed to us at the school gate. I remember reading it and this rush of emotion from my past hit me, the memory of the struggles I had and being taken out to be tested as mum was not happy with me being in a split class. As we walked home Hannah chatted away about the new classes for the next term, I asked her how she felt about it and she seemed happy with the friends she had in her class. I explained to her, it was not a case of the other class being better than her split class but that there were too many children there for just one class so therefore the classes had to be split. Hannah came back to me a few days later, she was upset and told me that there had been a discussion about the classes amongst her friends, and some were not happy with the split. Hannah said she had shared what I had told her about it not being that any one class was better than the other and one child snapped back at her, "my mum said your mum is upset and angry you are not in the older age class!!" Hannah was looking at me and she wanted to know if this was true. I remained calm and asked, "Hannah are you happy with your class?" she said "yes", I replied "so am I!!" It was in that moment I realised that everyone is fighting their own private battle of insecurities at the school gates we all have a story to tell, the things we find tough, our own memories of our time in school or our feelings of am I doing ok as a mum? And sometimes when we are all standing about waiting for our kids to come out of school, the tough day and the things we feel insecure about, just spills over.

Today looking at Hannah's journey in life, I know now what class she was in is irrelevant, I only see the young woman who at the age of 16, left school, chased her dreams and through hard work and determination, now runs her own business and has won an award for Scottish mobile hairdresser of the year at the age of 20. All our children are unique each with a plan and a destiny!!

The year Rebecca was to start school, I started saying to Ricky "do you think we should have another baby? I just don't feel like I am done yet". He would laugh and say, "we have no room in the car!!!" It was just after Christmas and we were due to go up North for the New Year, we were joining with mum, dad, my God parents their children, my brother and his family in a lodge to take in the New Year. We had been doing this for the last couple of years and it was like we got to live out the childhood dream I spoke about earlier, the one where we wondered what it would be like to all live together. For that one week of the year we got to do just that, and it was a lot of fun. This massive house in the Highlands of Scotland that had enough rooms to cater for us all, along with a large dining room and massive grounds to explore, we really do have some amazing memories form this time! My brother was always in charge of the fireworks, and he never lets us down, they were spectacular! Before going I was sorting out washing to get packed as we were leaving that night, and as I pulled the washing out of the machine the smell of the fabric softener made me feel sick, I thought "ahhh!!" Sure enough after going to get a test, it confirmed I was indeed pregnant! I told Ricky when he got in from work and we both started laughing, I said "well we were talking about it". We were both delighted but had decided not to tell anyone as we would enjoy it being our secret for a while. So, we headed off to the Highlands with the news tucked in our hearts that we were to become a family of six!! It was always a joy being back up North and the families always had fun we all took turns cooking. I was helping my dad and God dad in the kitchen as it was their turn this particular night, they had venison cooking in the oven and they asked me to check on it, as I opened the oven the smell hit me and I was transported back in time to the butchers kitchen with the smell of the ox tongue cooking! I had to make a dash to the toilet to throw up, mum had just come into the kitchen along with Ricky , she took one look at me as I rushed passed, turned to Ricky and said "is she pregnant?" so much for keeping it a secret!!

We Returned home, and with the news now told to the children, who were delighted, this pregnancy had a different feel to it. The girls were older and much more aware of what was going on. So, it felt like a whole family experience. They loved talking about the baby in my tummy and who was going to join the family. I was also now conquering the fear of the school gates; it didn't take up as much of my prayer life as before, however I did feel like God was challenging me to get involved in the parent council. I really battled with this and had many a conversation with Him about the reasons as to why I would be hopeless on the council! However, the time came around for the parent council annual general meeting and I could not ignore the prompting on the inside of me to be there, it just wouldn't go away. Our friends who lived in the village had told me they were going along so I thought "ok I can do it at least there will be a friendly face round the table". The first time I went, my heart was in my mouth, as we all sat, and introduced ourselves, I thought I might pass out with nerves, I just felt so out of my comfort zone and was having an all-out battle on the inside of me. But for some reason, being on the council just seemed really important and being a mum of two girls in school one in nursery and a baby on the way, I was going to be around school for some time. AS everyone spoke about what they did for a living, and who their children were and what class they were in, I realised the reason I didn't want to be involved in the first place was because I saw all these people with their fancy jobs and here I was just a housewife and mum. During the meeting my mouth was dry, I felt sick as it came to my turn to introduce myself, I prayed silently (as I was now used to the conversations with God around my insecurities), and out my of mouth, the words flowed confidently as I spoke of being a mum and housewife and who my girls were. God never let me down; I just wished the nerves were not so overwhelming at times! I was involved in the parent council for many years and found it was a place God used to strengthen me and grow my passion for the local school and community we were a part of, I was always happy to help and serve at coffee mornings and Christmas fares, I also developed the skill of face painting.

My pregnancy was passing quickly so with the months flying past, we needed to get ready! The girls were just so excited and with Rebecca starting school after the summer, change was coming to the Bain household! Three girls in school and a baby on the way! I was determined to enjoy the final months of having Rebecca at home to myself before she headed off to school and became a big sister, she would no longer be the baby of the family. I remember walking down the stairs with the washing and I heard worship music coming from the living room, there was a kids Hillsongs DVD playing, this was not unusual as our house was always full of worship music , it is the heart of who I am. As I came to the bottom of the stairs, I looked in through the glass living room door and there I could see Rebecca who was four years old standing with her hands in the air singing her heart out, eyes closed and oblivious to me watching. I sat on the stairs and watched this beautiful scene, I started to cry with a heart that was so overwhelmed at the sight of such pure worship. I thought, "If this was my heart how much more our father in heaven feels it when he sees, his children worship Him in that way". The whole scene caught my heart and took me yet again to a new place in my own worship.

As we prepared for the new baby life was busy, we were still very involved in church and community, and it was a great season. Ricky was great with the girls particularly on his Saturday off. He would take them swimming and to the park and give me a long lie and some rest time.... well mostly rest. He would often come home to find the house scrubbed from top to bottom or furniture moved!! Nesting was a thing for me!! True to form I was ten days over my due date, I was on worship singing on the Sunday and the next day I headed to the hospital with labour pains. I laboured through the night, things took a turn for the worse and I was moved from the midwives unit through to the labour ward as baby was in distress and my blood pressure was very low. I was given an epidural as they thought I may need a section. It was while I was getting my epidural that things went from bad to worse. I have a very vivid memory of this as I started to feel extremely unwell, I had never experienced this before, but I knew something was wrong. I could hear the emergency buzzer going and it was like I was floating away, I remember looking out the window at the clouds and thinking "they could just carry me away!!" I saw Ricky over on the other side of the room and the look on his face confirmed that things were not good so I tried to focus, I remember thinking "if I die he is going to be left all alone with the girls". This sudden rush of emotion along with the doctors' calm voice who was giving instructions to the team while all the time asking me questions kept my focus. He started asking me about the girls, what their names were, and how old they were. I was fighting the urge to just close my eyes and give up, I concentrated on his questions as the team worked around me, eventually my blood pressure started to come back up the doctor told Ricky they were giving me an hour to stabilise and then they were taking me down for a section. Ricky then phoned around asking people to start praying. He was extremely upset at what he had just witnessed; he knew I had only just pulled through! The epidural was working, and I was not in any pain, the team were prepping for me to go to theatre. I began to feel very agitated, I also felt a lot of pressure, the nurse that had come into the room said "I will just look and see what baby is doing", she started to get flustered and said "oh my word I can see the head!!!!" Again the buzzer rang for help, she didn't even get time to pull the bottom of the bed away to help deliver, and she only just got her gloves on in time as baby slipped out effortlessly with an arm out in front like a super hero!! The doctor was amazed as he had believed this would be a section delivery, but here she was, the fourth girl to join the Bain family! I could not believe my eyes, she was beautiful, and in that moment I was struck by her jet-black hair with these fine blond highlighted tips, I had never seen anything like it on a new-born baby. We had the name Naomi Rachel as a girl's name set aside, but as I looked at my beautiful baby girl, I knew her name was Rachel, so on the 25th August 2005 Rachel Naomi Bain was born. What a labour that was, a near death experience and then the miracle of not needing a section. I was emotionally and physically exhausted! I remained in hospital for a couple of days afterwards to recover. It was a wonderful moment when the excited older girls came to the hospital to meet their new sister. I have a photo of them all together with Ricky on that day and it is still one of my favourite photos! I bounced back quickly and was back at the school gates in no time showing off this gorgeous girl! Rachel just slotted into the family beautifully and the girls were such a great help and loving life with a new-born. The following Sunday I was back on stage doing what I love worshipping and singing, now with a new sense of being glad to be alive and thankful for the journey I was on. The faith I had and the love in my heart was so huge I could have burst with gratitude!! The family around us at church were amazing they kept an eye on Rachel as she sat in her car seat sleeping soundly as the worship team practiced. Ricky would arrive for church starting with the rest of the girls. While I carried Rachel in my tummy, she would come alive when I was singing; she would jump around on the inside of me. I remember when she was very small, around two years old, she would drum along using pens or anything she could find as her drumsticks, she would often dance around in worship; Rachel has an amazing gift of music on her life and from the womb I felt it.

People would often say to me "Joanne I have no idea how you do it, four girls and all the work you are involved in", I was thriving, and I would reply "I didn't get them all at once I worked up to it". This was so true, and I still believe that if you have three children you can have any amount, as by then you have mastered the skill of multitasking. The early stage with a new-born is always easy enough I found as they have arrived into our world so they must fit in. Rachel came most places with me, even along to parent council meetings, my nerves by this time were under wraps and I was less intimidated. The more children I had the more I loved it; I still saw it as a privilege. I also loved to organise and be a forward planner, the constant juggling kept me on my toes, but I loved it. The full diaries and school schedules, it was a full-time job that brought me so much joy and satisfaction, and a sense of fulfilment. Although I did work part time in this season; I was a childminder for some of the time while the children were growing up and at one point did some late shifts at Tesco. The girls loved the times I was on a late shift, they tell the story of when I'd go to work and Ricky was in charge. They knew he would get distracted watching football so they would get a late-night watching Scooby doo!! Mum was out so they had a free pass!! Things were tight with our ever-growing family and stretched finances, but Ricky and I were happy. We made the decision some years earlier that Ricky would not work offshore, this was offered to him on several occasions, but it was a core belief in both of us that it would be detrimental to our family. Sure, it was tempting, especially because with the offer of going away, came the offer of big money. But as we prayed for clarity, we always came back to the same conclusion in our hearts. Our lives were lived out for God and our hope was in Him the idea of Ricky working away did not fit with Gods plans and purposes for our life, our core foundational verse from Jeremiah 'I know the plans I have for you' is what always pulled our life towards the true North of where we were headed. I also mentioned previously about the many blessings God poured out on our lives, He saw our hearts that wanted to be obedient to his plan even through the struggles we faced. It was not always easy, and I am not about to make us out to be saints. Our finances were a tension, a source of arguments and frustrations that often boiled over. But there were times that God just blew us away, He sees it all, every struggle, every thought and emotion but every time we said, "your will be done Lord not ours!" Choices were made, that to this day we see the benefits in our grown children, who have a strong relationship with their dad because he was around and present, they are stronger because of this choice.

This one time, out of many where God chose to blow us away, we were at church and this couple approached us saying they wanted to buy us new sofas! I was speechless! They wanted to do it anonymously and did not want to be named, but could I go with them and pick what I wanted, and they would pay for it. I was overwhelmed; I had no words but agreed to go along with them to the shop. I felt so loved and I enjoyed every minute of that shopping experience, I couldn't believe the kindness of God s people to share what they had and to bless us, they had a heart that God used to bring His blessings to His people. This was love in a very practical way that touched my heart deeply. By now we were growing out of our house fast, it was time to pray for a new home again!

CHAPTER 9

THE FARM HOUSE

Rachel was a year old when we moved into the farmhouse in Echt, it was another house on Dunecht Estate and we were over the moon to get it! It was massive, the kitchen was my favourite place with its large dining table, there were five bedrooms, a living room and a garden that was huge! The kids were overjoyed with all this space to explore. It was up a farm track tucked in behind the trees, it was our little piece of heaven. Looking back at our time in the farmhouse, these were some of our hardest days, but this is not what we remember. The children to this day still reminisce about the adventures they got up to. I will never forget hearing about a story round our dinner table not that long ago when the girls told me about a game they used to play, I couldn't believe I was only just hearing about it then!! Our house was on a working farm and the fields that surrounded us had sheep in them, at the bottom of our garden over the wall was the first field and it had an electric fence. They used to play a game to see who could hold onto the fence the longest!! On one occasion the farmer had cows in the field, as they went to play the game, they all ended up being thrown back with the shock as the voltage had been turned up! Another time, they were playing on the bales of hay; Hannah fell down the middle of them upside down!! Thankfully they all managed to pull her out!! My heart was in my mouth as I heard these stories for the first time; they all howled with laughter as they reminisced about their adventures. This was a home that was filled with love, laughter, tears, noise, fun and lots of friends to visit. I feel very blessed to have had the time living there. We rented our home and although we struggled at times, I would talk to God about this as everyone was on about how it's good to buy a home. This was not something we were in a position to do, but we felt that the rent we paid was not wasted money but an investment into a lifestyle in the country that was giving our children an upbringing we could never have afforded otherwise. With our large family and the rent being affordable we were happy and mostly at peace, anytime I had a pang of 'ahhh we are not normal we should be owning a house' I would offer my prayer to God and He would bring me His peace as we truly were in the plan that He had for us, and we loved where we were.

The house was a great place to entertain and to host our community group. Ricky was asked to lead a community Group along with this other lady in our church, I was so upset that I was not asked to do it with him, and I can honestly say this was one of the most painful things ever as a young wife. I was desperate for Ricky and me to do something together as this had always been my heart's desire, we did plenty separately for God but to do something together would have been awesome. This took some prayer to manage, as there were meetings I was not included in, with the insecurities in my own heart about my identity, this almost tipped me over the edge! Poor Ricky took the brunt of a lot of my negative vibes about this. I would pour out my heart to God in my bath at the end of the day, this became my time out to ponder the day and discuss the pains I had in my heart. I concluded that the leaders in the church had made this decision so it must be right, and I would just have to trust. But it was very hard and left me feeling that I was not enough and not good enough to partner with my own husband and that another woman had to do it!! I remember one of the times in my bath praying and asking God to help me. I saw in my mind a picture of hurdles and I felt that God was saying life was going to be full of hurdles, but I would learn to jump over them with Him and that sometimes I would clear them and it would be easy, with others I would clip my foot and maybe even stumble, but I was to get back up and keep running, take each hurdle as they approached with confidence in who God was, and that he had a plan and it was a good one!!

Our involvement in the church and in the village kept us busy, I was now leading the women's bible study group BIBS as well as being part of the worship team. With four girls there was never a dull moment, but we loved it, I thrived on the busyness! Friday would come round and it would be sweety day and movie night, more often than not the girls would have their friends round for a sleepover, although Ricky used to say "I don't know why you call it a sleep over as no one sleeps!!"

Over the years, despite my difficulties in school when I was younger, I found a love for reading. I loved to read all sorts of books but Christian books about other people's stories were my favourite. We had a library bookshelf in the church, one Sunday I was browsing through it and came across a Book called Supernatural Ways of Royalty by Kris Vallotton, I was intrigued and took it home and started reading it. There are moments in our life that I call 'stake in the ground moments' when things happen, and your life is forever changed. Reading this book was one of those times as I started on a journey of discovering my identity. A journey, that took me to an understanding of how God sees me and His thoughts about me. I was just so caught up in how much I loved God and how much He helped in my everyday life; I had never considered what He thought of me. I knew He loved me because of what He had done by sending Jesus to the cross to die for me. But as I read the book and had light bulb moment after light bulb moment, as I learned about our thinking and how it needs to match Gods thinking about us, about walking in confidence of who God says we are, it was like God was taking off the layers of insecurity. One by one, all the lies I had believed about myself were starting to be stripped away and He began replacing them with the truths of who He says I am. This was life changing! It was also around this time that a visiting pastor was invited to come to our church, and I would experience another of those moments where I was forever changed. The pastor was Alan Ross, a prophet, I had no idea what a prophet was, but as I sat and listened to him, I was captivated by his story. He was an alcoholic living on the streets of Glasgow when God got hold of his life and completely transformed it. He now travels the world praying for people and telling them how God sees them. At the end when he had finished telling his story he said he would like to pray over a few people. Ricky and I were chosen and as we walked out to the front to be prayed for, my heart was racing, I prayed silently in my heart saying, "God I feel nervous, and I just want to know it's you and that I am doing well". The first words out of Alan's mouth as he prayed over me were "daughter, well done good and faithful servant" my heart on the inside exploded!! The power that hit me that night has never left me and along with the full prophetic word he spoke over Ricky and I has been a source of deep encouragement even to this day. We had lovely friends at this time that came around us and joined our journey, they spent a lot of time with us, and we spent many a night around the big table after a meal chatting into the wee small hours. Having trusted friends to share with and bounce ideas off is vital and these friends we cherish and thank God for them.

Having baths became my time out, I would have one every evening and would often be on the phone as sometimes it was the only place I got peace to talk in our busy house. I would chat to my friend; she was a great sounding board as I navigated my way through finding my identity, throwing off the layers of lies and speaking out the truths. I will be forever thankful for the many, many, Conversations, as she answered my questions, we laughed and cried together!! Life is not all a bed of roses, the Bible even tells us we will not always have an easy life, but God promises to be with us in all we go through.

Our table in the kitchen was a very special place in the farmhouse, and today the table is still a key place in our home. We've had many people sitting round it, some of whom God brought our way as we offered a place of safety as they weathered their own storms and some, he brought to encourage us. It was a place where friendship and family came together. It was always the place we would hold family meetings, as running a family of six was a full-time job. As I navigated my way through being a mum to four growing girls with such different but strong personalities, my faith grew and was stretched with the changing dynamics in the family. As the children were growing up, I relied on the gentle nudge from the Holy Spirit when navigating parenting. A lot of my ideas on how to manage would come to me as I was about my daily chores in the house, and I remember having the idea of the family meeting round the table. Most meetings were called on the back of a behaviour that needed to be reined in! It was a place where they would all get to discuss what their thoughts on a particular grievance were, or where Ricky and I would get to express our disappointment on how they were all treating each other. We would always finish by bringing it back to what God says we would pray as a family and bring to God the things we had been discussing. God was at the centre of our lives; Ricky and I prayed that the children would know Him from a young age and have their own faith, not just because we believed or because they were raised in a Christian home but that they would have a personal experience of who he was to them.

We now had a seven-seater car, we had purchased this after Rachel was born, I said to Ricky one day "we'll we have a spare seat in the car, shall we have another baby?" I think he thought I was joking but I knew years ago that God had told Ricky He would give him a son. So, I knew he wouldn't take much convincing!! I remember praying for Samuel by name and asking God to bless us with him. I asked for His will to be done in our lives. I loved being a mum to the girls and I would equally have loved another one, but it was a question with every pregnancy, people would ask me "oh are you hoping for a boy?" The answer was always, "I am excited to see who gets to join our family". It was not long before we called a family meeting to announce that we were going to have a new baby join our family!! After all it would be a shame to waste the spare seat in the car!! My pregnancy was great, I felt amazing and had loads of energy. I was also aware this was going to be my last one, so wanted to enjoy it.

The months passed and as the due date approached and I prepared my hospital bag, I really wanted to buy a blue baby grow and pack it but I thought that Ricky would think I asked at one of the scans what we were having, as we had agreed not to find out, so, I just packed a white one, but deep in my heart I knew I was having my Samuel. One Sunday at Church, Tommy MacNeil a minister from Lewis and his wife Donna were visiting, he was preaching and was fantastic I loved the service. At the end I was just enjoying the worship when Tommy's wife came over to me and asked could she pray for me, I was overjoyed and said, "yes of course". She said that she saw a Hannah anointing over me, (now Hannah was a woman in the Bible who was infertile and asked for a son and she called him Samuel.) Tommy had been preaching on the river of God and how some people were standing at the edge watching, and others were paddling in it, some were venturing farther in, he put out an invitation as God was calling us to go deep into His River. She said to me that I was someone who was up to my neck in the river, but I was not there alone, she saw ducklings five or six of them. I was so blessed by what she had said as she didn't even know me; I had never met her before. But she noticed I was pregnant and I went on to tell her I had four children already! It was such an encouraging time for me as the cry of my heart was to raise the children in a way that they would see who God was. That it's not just a case of, 'this is what we do as Christians, follow rules and a structure', but it's a way of life and God is real. This one picture of the ducklings in the river with me encouraged my heart as I knew it was God giving me a visual representation of where we were at.

Excitement in the Bain family was growing as baby was almost here! I was still serving on the Parent Council and the day before my due date the school was having a disco. As I was always ten days overdue with all my other pregnancies I thought I would be fine to help out. The disco was in full swing, and I was on the tuck shop, I started to feel those first twinges but brushed them off as Braxton Hicks. However, they were not settling down, so I said to one of the other mums that I was going to head to a friend's house who lived a few doors away from the village hall where the disco was being held and that I would get Ricky to pick the girls up later. I was walking down the road and had to stop every so often to let the pain pass! I eventually arrived at my friend's house; I was quite flustered gripping the door frame as I rang the bell. When she came to the door and saw me, she couldn't believe it, as a few months earlier she'd had a dream that I had given birth in her kitchen! She did not hang about, she phoned for Ricky to take me to hospital as there was no way she wanted to be delivering a baby!! We still laugh about this now and the horror she felt when I had arrived at her door in full labour! Samuel was born in the early hours of the morning on the 15th of March 2008. He was born with the cord around his neck and lifeless. He was immediately taken away and rushed to resus, Ricky was told to stay where he was, but I was shouting to Ricky "go after them, go after them", so he rushed down the corridor, he then heard the sound we were desperate to hear, the shrill of the new-born cry!! The nurse put her head round the door to say, "he is fine we are just giving him oxygen." It was not long till he was back and in my arms. I couldn't take my eyes off him, as I spoke to my Samuel for the first time welcoming him into the world and saying, "we have prayed for you, it's so good to finally meet you." News spread fast around the labour ward about the lady who had just given birth to a boy after having four girls. Many of the staff popped in to say "hi" and to meet Samuel. By the time I made it up on to the ward the news had travelled to them too and they had a private side room waiting for me. I had been in hospital many times and this had never happened before I felt like a celebrity!!! The nurse said to me "we had this room free and wanted you to have it, with five children you deserve some peace and rest before you head home." It was such a lovely thing to do. The girls soon arrived, excited to meet their baby brother. Over the next couple of days I had a steady stream of visitors; all excited to meet Samuel he caused quite a stir. It was great to finally get home and start our lives as a family of seven. Samuel was a sleepy baby, and I was feeding him myself as I had done with all the others. The health visitor who I had known for some years now was coming in most days as Samuel's weight was dropping and showing no signs of coming back up. She told me if things didn't improve, they would need to take him back into hospital to see what was going on. I was exhausted, I was functioning on very little sleep and fear was nipping at my heart. I had this horrible sense that something was going to happen to him and I couldn't shake it off. Over the next couple of days, I was over thinking everything. I wasn't able to go to bed at night; I stayed downstairs on the sofa with Samuel right beside me in his cradle. I would jump at every sound he made until eventually, I was a blubbering wreck, sleep deprivation had kicked in and my emotions were all over the place!

My parents, having moved down from Tain were now living in Aberdeenshire so my mum was around to help. I also had some support and prayer from friends as I tried to work out why I was feeling so overwhelmed. I had fed four other babies no problem, why was this happening with Samuel? My Mum came in one morning and said "Jojo I was praying for Samuel last night and I saw him as a strong grown Man, he is going to be fine" This brought peace to my heart, and I made the decision to switch from breast to bottle as Samuel was taking from the bottle better, and the constant expressing was exhausting so switched him to formula. I started to feel my strength return and clarity of thought as I made decisions around what was best for Samuel and me, and for the rest of the family. I remember the night I took Samuel upstairs to sleep for the first time, I placed him in his Moses basket and thanked God for him, the child I had asked for by name, and I thanked Him that He had a plan, and it was a good one!! I kicked fear in the teeth, climbed into my bed and went to sleep. For the first time since Samuel had been born I was at peace. There are many things sent to rob us of our peace and fear is one thing the enemy of our soul will use, but it's only effective if we give into it. I love the passion translation Bible and in psalm 23 (one of my favourite psalms) verse 4 says "Fear will never conquer me, for you already have!!!" God has me and as He has shown me many times, the children were His before they were ever mine and his love far outweighs my earthly love. That's a safe place to rest in!!

The years in the farmhouse stand out to us as a family and we still talk about our time there. We saw many day-to-day unexpected God moments where He showed up, whether it was a visit from friends at just the right moment when a cuppa and a chat was needed, or a bag of shopping left at the door, food made and brought to us at times when we had no money for shopping. They had no idea how significant it was to listen to the small voice prompting them to bring food. All stories that you could look at and say, "what a coincidence", but I know that my Heavenly Father heard the cry of my heart and answered. These times I believe, were our training ground for the life of faith Ricky and I walk now. In that house, in the wee small hours is where I learned to push in, to sit with the word of God and ask questions about the things that were on my heart. I was amazed at what the Holy Spirit would reveal to me through the Bible. If you have never picked up the Bible or have not done so for some time, I challenge you to sit quietly, ask God some questions you have on your heart and open the word of God that is as alive today as the day it was written. You will be amazed at what treasures you will find.

As we struggled in those days and money was tight, I would pray "Lord don't let this affect our children". As we sit round our family table and hear the children tell tales of the farmhouse, this prayer is more than answered because they tell it as an adventure and how much of an amazing childhood they had, the freedom of friends staying and the endless tales of hilarity! I love listening to them chat together, my heart is full as I look at them now as young adults. Tough life events don't define us they become part of our story. The choice is how we see our story; it depends on the lenses we look through.

We were in the farmhouse for seven years; the children were growing up and Katie and Hannah were now in the Academy which meant I spent a lot of time on the road between Echt and Alford. One day while the older girls were at dancing, I was walking through the village after getting ice cream. Samuel was in the buggy and Rachel and Rebecca were walking beside me, it was a normal sunny day and we were on our way back up to the school to collect the girls before heading home. As I walked up Greystone Road, I heard the words "I will give you the land your feet walk on"; it stopped me in my tracks! I asked to God "are you moving us to Alford?" This was another life altering moment that changed our lives forever! As I drove home, I couldn't stop thinking about it and later when the kids were in bed I tried to find in the Bible where these words were, I found them in the book of Joshua. Over the next few weeks, I kept thinking about what had happened but had not yet told Ricky. One Sunday night after the children were in bed, we were sitting in the living room and Ricky said to me "Alford would be a good place to live don't you think?" I could not believe it, I replied "you will never guess what I heard when I was walking there the other day", so I told him exactly what had happened. We talked about whether it was a possibility or not. We turned on the computer and searched 'houses for rent in Alford.' There was one house that had just been listed, we agreed we would phone in the morning and set up a viewing and leave it with God to direct our path if this was where we were meant to be. Ricky and I were the first people to view this house on Burnbank Road. From the moment we walked through the doors we knew this was going to be our new home, but we also knew... we did not have the money for the deposit. We had to decide there and then if we wanted it as there was going to be a day of viewings and we knew this house would be snapped up. In that moment Ricky and I looked at each other and said, "let's do this!!"

The events that unfolded over the next few weeks blew us away; our faith was stretched as we had never walked anything like this before. We signed for a house knowing we didn't have the money for the deposit, but we knew in our hearts this was God, He was in it, and we trusted him to provide. We only told a couple of trusted praying friends what we were doing and what we felt God was asking us to do. I can honestly say this was an experience that will never leave me as we both, as a couple had to push past fear completely, look to God stand on His word and not give into the over whelming voice screaming at us "what are you doing!!!" I have the date marked in my Bible, the day one of the friends we told phoned me and said, "I have a verse from God for you regarding the house, it's In 1 John chapter 5 verses 14 and 15". I have underlined it and written beside it, 'for the house', here is what it says... 'This is the confidence we have in approaching God, that if we ask anything according to his will, he will hear us. And if we know that he hears us whatever we ask we know that we have what we asked for'. I knew in my heart that if this was Gods will then this would happen and if not, I was confident in whom He was and the plan He had for us. The money we needed came in from three different sources; the last amount was given to us the night before the deposit needed to be paid. It was an incredible miracle of Gods provision and an incredible journey that stretched our faith. We were now moving to Alford, and we were slap bang in the middle of Gods plan for our lives. What an adventure!!

CHAPTER 10

A MOTHERS HEART

Being a mum to five children, I have always said "if I do nothing else with my time here on earth, being a mum is enough, they will always be my greatest achievement". They have helped me grow as a person, filled my heart with a love that I never thought possible and taken me on a journey deeper into the heart of who God is because of my role as a mother. God taught me early on that they were a gift from Him, and He knew them by name before I did. This always brought my heart back to the true North when I felt overwhelmed with the task ahead of me, particularly in the teenage years. I am grateful for the Holy Spirit who was a constant help in times of crisis, and there were many I can assure you!

When Ricky was celebrating his 50th Birthday we were getting photos taken as a family, someone came up to me afterwards and said "well-done you have done an amazing job, that does not just happen, that has taken a lot of hard work!" From one mother's heart to another we connected in that moment. It is easy to look on at people's lives, especially now where everything is 'newsworthy' on social media, and we can think what a great life they lead, while never fully understanding what is behind the picture. But as two mothers' hearts connected, we understood the cost involved in raising children and giving them a firm foundation to then go on and build their own lives.

From a young age I have always loved Wonder Woman, I watched as a young girl and was captivated by this superhero who was a woman, and even now the modern-day Wonder Woman is just as awesome. I would say my inner mother is definitely Wonder Woman. In the movie she wears on her wrist Bracelets of Submission; she uses them as her primary method of defence, deflecting gun fire, blasts and small missiles, a bit like raising teenagers in my experience! While they have been raised with the knowledge and understanding of who God is and have witnessed Him at work in our lives as well as experiencing Him for themselves, they still had to live their lives and experience what the world had to offer and make their choices. As a Mother I had to help direct them without being a dictator and only having them do what I wanted them to be involved in. As sometimes it's through our mistakes that we learn, I know this to be true as I made many mistakes myself, but these life lessons have helped me become the woman I am today. My famous saying as my children left the house to go out was always "make good choices!" It was a phrase that became very familiar to all their friends who were around, and I was nicked named by the girls' friends as 'Mamma Bain!!'

Making good choices was an area I would use the defence bracelets as the girls would talk openly about parties they wanted to go to, or other events including sleepover's, things that would often pull them away from church life. As we discussed this together, I would see how their requests hit my spirit- at times it would be a yes whereas other times it would be a firm no!! I would see myself using the bracelets as hitting away any potential missiles to protect them. I wanted them to experience life and make choices for themselves, but I wanted to protect them too. Ricky was a street pastor at the time when the older girls were teenagers, and he would speak to many people in an evening who had grown up in the church but no longer attended, they would say to him "I have no time for church or God!" As we discussed these conversations together we would find it all very sad and I would say "I don't ever want the girls to feel like that." This is why we discussed their choices and allowed them the freedom to choose while having firm boundaries in place to protect them. We encouraged them to pray about things and come back to us when they had, teaching them that it's their relationship with God and that He speaks to them about them, He knows them the best. But being teenagers this was not always easy for them and often we would not agree. I would often sit in the children's rooms when they were out at school and pray for them, it was during one of these times when I had a real sense that one of them was having a hard time a school with bullying and I was able to speak to her about it. The Holy Spirit truly is amazing at revealing things to us when we ask.

We had an understanding with them that no topic was off limits, anything could be talked about, and we had some very interesting chats covering many topics! I always said to them "tell the truth, we can work with anything if it's the truth, and it helps if I hear it from you guys first as I don't want to hear what you're up to from someone else at the school gates!!"

Another time I was using my inner Wonder Woman parenting style, was in the form of 'the rope of truth'. Looking back I now see this very much as the Holy Spirit bringing light on a situation to bring the truth out. One of the girls came home very upset, she had already spoken to her sister and so they had come to find me to explain what had happened. A young lad from the village had read the over friendliness of her as a green light to take her to the woods and try his luck with her. She was so upset at what had happened and was feeling very uncomfortable. I felt sick to my stomach, but as always the Holy Spirit was quick to prompt me with a plan. I told her that her Dad and I were going to pay this young lad and his family a visit. She was hysterically objecting and to be honest I was thinking to myself "are you sure this is a good plan God!!" But one of our core values as a family is to bring things into the light, when they are brought out of the darkness the enemy of our soul has no power, I knew this story could grow arms and legs in a small village. So, Ricky and I headed off to see the family, we knew them but not very well. In the car on the way round we prayed, and as we knocked on the door my heart was racing. We went inside and explained what had just happened and that we had come to discuss it and to make sure this was not played out on social media. We explained how upset our daughter was and that this could not happen again! The mum was lovely and very understanding, she said we will be round just shortly, and my son will apologise. They came past the house, and he was deeply sorry. We had a good discussion that was helpful to both of them. They left and I felt such relief. Another incoming missile deflected by bringing it into the light it was no longer a story that would grow arms and legs, but a victory in the journey of raising teenagers. Sometimes the choices we make lead us onto hard situations but by taking a deep breath and facing it head on it becomes a part of the story and journey of a life lived in victory and not in the shadows of fear.

Being a parent is an emotional roller coaster, there are times that it takes my breath away and at other times it breaks my heart. One of the hardest times as a parent is when you can't help your children when they are struggling. One of the girls suffered terrible bullying in school; I had been at school many times and been in countless meetings to try to navigate the way through. I have sat and hugged them as they cried tears of pain and angry shouts of "where is God in all of this, why is this happening to me?" As a parent you want to take the pain away, but life is full of things that are way out of our control and our children must find their own way through the storm. One day as I was busy in the kitchen making dinner and slightly distracted, Rebecca came in and said, "mum can I show you something", I replied "sure" only half listening as I concentrated on cooking the dinner. But as she started to speak and share what had just happened as she sat in her bedroom, my heart pulled my full attention to what she was saying. She was crying as she explained how upset she was about all that had been happening with her friends. She put on You Tube to listen to her favourite worship song at the time called Lead Me to The Cross, on the screen came a clip from the movie The Passion of the Christ and the song was played over it. She showed it to me on her laptop, she said "I had never really thought about what Jesus had gone through mum, and seeing this made it all real, he went through this for me!" She then told me what Jesus had said on the cross, "forgive them Father for they do not know what they have done". She explained "it hit me mum, these girls that have been mean to me have no idea how they have made me feel, and I need to forgive them, as what I am going through is nothing compared to what Jesus went through". By now we were both crying. I was so proud of Rebecca in that moment and absolutely blown away with the love of God as He had taken her on a journey in her own room and helped her to forgive her friends. It was such a beautiful moment. Forgiveness is the key in our journey of faith and Rebecca had learned it all on her own, just her and God in her room. A powerful choice to forgive that set her free, the situation did not change, life was still hard but with the freedom she had in her heart she felt different, her perspective had completely changed.

I now understood that not only did God have a plan for my life but equally he had one for each of the children. The verse in Jeremiah that God spoke to me as a young girl was now a foundational verse in our family, we often quoted it at times of uncertainty, and we would pray together as a family asking God to bring about his plans for our lives. When my oldest daughter Katie was getting ready to leave school, she wanted to join the police, but she'd had so much advice from the school and other police officers saying she should go to university first they said she was too young to join the police, and they probably wouldn't take her at 18, as they like people to have life experience first. She came home from school upset and not sure what to do as she had good grades and could have gone to university, if that's what she wanted. We talked about what it was she really wanted to do, and her answer was clear "mum I only want to join the police, and anyway God has a plan!!" Katie applied for the police and was accepted she was the youngest officer in her intake! Ricky and I were so proud of her for going after what she had on her heart and not being influenced by others thoughts and opinions.

One of our favourite things to do on a Saturday night as a family was to get a takeaway and watch a movie. Ricky came home one evening after being down the main street to pick up a Chinese carry out and said to me "I have just walked past a house for sale on the main street Joanne, do you fancy taking a look?" "Absolutely not!" came my reply "I love the house we have I am very happy here!!" He explained that he had walked past the house with the lion door knocker and as he was looking at it he heard God say, "this is your house!!" He eventually convinced me to go and view it, but I felt confident as we were not in a position to buy a house and thought it was just a flash in the pan thing, surely God wasn't moving us again!! We made the appointment and went for the viewing. I wandered around the house and in my head was saying "this is awful, there is no way I want to live here"; my heart attitude was not good!! As we walked home and discussed it I said to Ricky "you got it wrong no way are we living there". Over the next couple of days I could not get peace, I was restless and was not sure why. I finally went to prayer with what was going on on the inside of me, avoiding the house issue! I eventually took my bad attitude before God and along with the schedule for the house I sat in prayer. I looked at it and read the words 'we offer up for sale in the heart of the community', I felt God pull at my spirit and say "I want you in the heart of this community!!" I went back to Ricky and said "I think you are right God does want us in that house, we better go back and view it again!!" Against all the odds; because on paper we really should not have been granted a mortgage, after a roller coaster of a journey we were able to purchase the house! God often makes a way where there seems to be no way!! And to this day we are still living in the house in the heart of the community, as couple with Gods heart for the community firmly on our hearts.

I was lying in my bath one evening thanking God, as for the first time in what seemed like for ever we had two wages coming into our house and for once we could see a light at the end of the tunnel of our constant lack of finance. As I was praying and releasing my thanks and resting in the comfort those two wages brought, I felt an uneasy feeling in the pit of my stomach. I did think it was weird as normally when I am thanking God the opposite is the case and I am flooded with peace. I now know it was a warning as three days later I was sitting having my lunch when Ricky phoned me, "Joanne start praying I have been called to the board room and it's not looking good". The rush of emotion hit the pit of my gut with a thud; I put my head in my hands straightaway to start praying against Ricky losing his job. I could feel the fight mode rise up on the inside of me and I was ready to do battle!! But as my head hit my hands I heard very clearly a line from one of my favourite songs, 'my hope is built on nothing less than Jesus blood and righteousness', in that came a challenge to me; 'Joanne where is your hope?!' As the tears fell I prayed Lord my hope is in you, not in the oil industry. As I surrendered to the will of God in our lives, I started to thank God for His plan for our lives and that He knew what the future held!! Ricky arrived home a few hours later and as he told me the news that he had indeed been made redundant... We cried. But as a couple we trusted that God had a plan and it was a good one!!

My children inspire me and help me to be brave and try new things. After moving to the village of Alford when the children started getting older and going to the academy, I had taken a job in the local Bistro at the weekends. The extra cash was great and I wanted to get to know people in the village. We knew God had moved us to the village and we were keen to find out what he had for us to do. We had it in our hearts to plant a church but as we prayed and asked God what was next, we both felt we needed to just get involved in the community and get to know people first, and for people get to know who Ricky and Joanne were! I loved the work at the bistro, it was such a laugh with the girls I worked with, and with the people that came in for meals, and I felt like I was on their nights out too!! During my time there Hannah and Katie also joined the team for a time. I was also now involved in the Alford Primary Parent Council and Ricky was coaching the boys' football team. We adored our life and this little village in the heart of Aberdeenshire along with the people in it captured our hearts.

After a couple of years, I got the opportunity to work for the local council at the ski centre as part of the leisure team. So, it was time to leave the Bistro and move on to start a new adventure. In the months that followed I did my NPLQ to become a lifeguard, this was so far out of my comfort zone and a huge challenge, not just physically but mentally as well. The children were amazing and my biggest cheerleaders!! The training was gruelling, and I had many bruises from climbing in and out of the pool! There was dry work and pool work, we had to complete an exam and various tests in the water, where we would have to race against the clock to swim out to our casualties and then tow them back to the side. One of the scariest parts of the exam for me was the dive we had to make to go get the body from the bottom of the pool, this had to be done on the first attempt, failure to do so on the day of the exam meant you failed everything!! This became a huge deal for me, and the nerves were so over whelming. I was doing my training at the Aboyne pool so the drive back and forth was good for me, it helped me focus and pray, I was determined to pass this!! This was the first time in many years I had done something that was totally about me, Joanne, not Joanne the mum, wife, church leader or the many other titles I had. It was quite overwhelming as I was comfortable in all the other roles I had, but this was scary and was pushing me to the limits. As I prayed and spoke out in the car journeys declaring "I can do this!! I am strong enough!" I wanted to make my husband and children proud; there is a scripture in the Bible that says "I can do all things through Christ who strengthens me" this is found in Philippians chapter 4 verse 13. Part of the journey of faith and understanding our identities in Christ is to not just say the verses from the Bible but to put them in to practice! So, as I would stand at the poolside waiting for the whistle to blow so I could start the timed swim, or the moment I would dive down for the body to lift it from the bottom, as I reached out to grab it I would push past the rising fear and the panic that wanted to overtake my thoughts and tell me "you can't do it!!!" I would scream at myself under the water "you can do it, you can do it" over and over! I would imagine the body at the bottom was one of my children and swim like their lives depended on it! The day I passed my NPLQ was incredible it gave me such a sense of achievement! I have suffered most of my life from feeling inadequate and not good enough; feelings of failure would haunt me from my childhood. But on this day, it was so much more than just passing a test. I had just conquered years of feeling like a failure and being scared to push myself, in that moment another layer of lies that I believed about myself was removed.

I was now a fully qualified Lifeguard and working at the Alford swimming pool. One morning as I came down off the high chair at the poolside to let my colleague on, I thought to myself "what a real privilege to sit up high and guard the lives of the people of Alford as they swim". As I walked back to the staff room I knew the call on my life was not just to do this in the natural but in the supernatural as well, as I prayed for this village and the people in it.

The heart I have as a mother does not just stop at my own children, the way God has shaped it and made me, has me crying out in prayer for the children and young people of the village. One day in particular after one of my girls came home from school asking to go to yet again another house party, my heart sank. The constant navigating of this season of house parties was taking its toll! Don't get me wrong, I love a good party, but the age at which they were starting to attend seemed to be getting younger and younger and alcohol was readily available! Because they live rurally and not in the city where there are other options like ice skating, going to the cinema or out for food together, this was not so accessible. We seem to have created a culture where it is acceptable to allow young teenagers to be drinking and partying like they were 18, Childhoods being cut short, because other options are not on their doorsteps. Over the years I would regularly take a car load of teenagers into town to a youth group, ice-skating or the cinema to soften the blow when I said "no" to yet another party. One day when driving in the car by myself I was praying about this, I was crying real tears and shouting at God "there must be more than this for our young people?" It was during this prayer time that the heart for Alford Youth Cafe was born, (now widely known as AYC). When I arrived home I tearfully told Ricky what happened on my car journey. He caught the vision as I told him of the building God had shown me that we could run a cafe from for the young people. Over the coming months we gathered together some like minded people and we met on a weekly basis to first pray, and then plan. Eight month after that car journey, Alford Youth cafe opened its doors for the first time! The vision was clear, to provide a safe, friendly fun environment for young people of academy age to come and hang out on a Friday night. Our hearts were to see the teenagers in the community build friendships and solid foundations as they moved into adulthood.

It was not long before my boss was encouraging me to go and do the swimming teachers course, I thought about it for a bit and then decided to go for it!! It became my favourite part of the job, the thrill of teaching complete non swimmers to swim and to see them progress over the weeks was amazing. I taught the adult and child class as well as the preschool, primary age and the adults' classes. I also taught one to one with children with various life challenges whether it was health related or ASD (Autism Spectrum Disorder). I loved all aspects of the job, the variety of the age range and abilities stretched me as a teacher. I had some great colleagues whom I learned a lot from, and over the years I became a confident teacher. Teaching people to swim is very similar to a life lived in faith; I have seen many similarities over the years. The young child splashing around looking confident in and out of the water, splashing and not paying attention! But as they have very little knowledge and understanding of swimming they are actually a danger to themselves and others, one slip and they fall under or worse grab onto another child and take them down too. Then there is the terrified swimmer who clings to the side of the pool refusing to let go. But you also get the child who trusts what you're saying while looking straight at you, holding their float and doing exactly as you say "keep kicking don't stop, look ahead don't panic, breath, chin on the water and blow bubbles". The role of the teacher is to move among the class gaining trust from all levels of ability, to get them to focus and relax and listen to the instructions. The key is not to give too many so as not to overwhelm the pupil. The life of faith can be like this, as we have to keep our eyes fixed on Jesus. If we are over confident in our own ability we can get ourselves into tricky situations, or if we are living in fear we end up going nowhere! But if we focus on the still small voice we can move forward in confidence knowing who holds the future. This is good to remember as I navigate my mother's heart through this season of letting my children go, with one married and one to be married in the next few weeks. The pain of saying goodbye to a season I have loved and letting go of being the main person in their life can be overwhelming. Fear can often grip your heart and cause you to have unhealthy expectations of your children as they make the transition from being children under your roof to adults making their own choices in the world. What this looks like for me, is making the transition from parenting in the natural to the supernatural as I continue to pray for them and be their biggest cheerleader. I have found the joy in letting go and seeing them become the awesome adults they are today!

A few years ago it was highlighted due to spending so much time in the water my life was now becoming directly affected by my monthly cycle, I had suffered for years but due to the nature of my job now, this was getting in the way of it. I had been back and forwards to the doctors now several time and was given some awful medication that had stopped my cycle all together! The side effects of this medication made my body think I was menopausal with all the symptoms, like hot flushes and mood swings! I remember saying to Ricky "I really don't feel like myself, nothing about what I feel or think sounds like me, I don't like me very much!!" I would say to him and the children "at least you get to walk away, I am stuck with me!!" This was really a tough period for us as a couple and looking back I am so thankful to Ricky, he really did stand by me and love me well during this time. After a year I had an appointment with the consultant at the hospital where it was decided that a hysterectomy was the best course of action. In the summer of 2019, I was taken in for the operation. It was major surgery and I was feeling slightly nervous. I remember on the days leading up to the operation praying and asking God for his peace to settle my fears. I sat on my bed one morning speaking to God and explaining my overwhelming concerns about the operation, but as I sat there I could feel his love and peace calm my heart and in that moment I knew it would all be fine. These are not just some fluffy words I write about to say "it will all be ok", but a true experience that only the love of the Father can bring. When we talk about real fears it's hard to feel the peace, you can try to push them down and pretend all is well but to truly give over the things that are causing you concern to the One who formed you in your mother's womb, that's faith. If you are reading thinking "aye right!!" I challenge you to open up the lines of communication with God through prayer; your life will never be the same again, trust me!! The operation was a success although it took slightly longer as they ended up taking everything out, a total hysterectomy! I was in hospital for around four days and then off work for around three months to recover. It was a slow process which was quite frustrating, but I was thankful to the family and friends around me as. I recovered they visited, brought food and generally helped out while I was off my feet. After around six weeks I went to the doctor's for an appointment to receive my results and get a general check up to see how I was doing. It was just an ordinary day as I walked along to the surgery was enjoying the fine weather. I waited to be called and headed in to see the doctor. I sat down as he was studied his computer screen, the room was quiet for a few moments causing me to shift in my seat; I wasn't concerned but started to feel nervous at his silence. He must have sensed my apprehension and said "don't worry Joanne it's not bad news there were no cancer cells detected" I was relieved, but what came next made time stand still in my mind for several moments. He explained the results and commented that he was shocked with what they diagnosed me with, as this was a diagnosis for women with infertility issues!! The doctor knew I had five children so as I sat there letting it sink in I asked him "are you saying my children are miracles?!" He gently replied "it looks that way" As I slowly walked home with my heart absorbing this, I started to cry, I was so overwhelmed I thought my heart was going to burst. I just kept saying "thank you" over and over again to God, I could not believe it!! My body could not have done this on its own I had medical evidence that I should not have had children, yet here I was with five miracles. My mother's heart was so thankful and to this day this still takes my breath away, I am so thankful to God. As I told Ricky I said to him "do you remember when I said to you all those years ago there is something special about our children and you said all parents feel like that?" I explained to him "I knew it was so!! Our children are special Ricky as they should not be here; my body could not have done it!!!" BUT GOD......

CHAPTER 11

THE YEAR THE WORLD STOPPED

I was now back at work and teaching again, life was good!!! My mum and dad had sold their house in town and had now bought a house out in Alford. This was great news; they would be within walking distance and with family life so busy it was great that they would be nearby. They were now both retired and decided to go to Lanzarote for a month to celebrate, towards the end of their stay we started hearing about this virus called Corona, I didn't think too much about it but when they arrived home I was relieved that they made it back as we were now hearing about hotels closing and guests being stranded without flights to get home! Mum and dad were now packing up their house and getting ready for the move to Alford, because it was a brand new house they bought, they had asked if they could they come and stay with us for a couple of weeks until they had organised flooring and blinds etc. We were delighted to have them as I have a great relationship with my parents and enjoy hanging out with them and so does Ricky. Moving day arrived and their belongings went into storage for what we thought would be a couple of weeks. The day after they moved into our house the entire county went into lockdown!! The whole thing was surreal!! Like the rest of the nation we were glued to the TV for news reports... and all the rules. We joked with mum and dad and said "we just didn't want them to be lonely in retirement, so we were all joining them!!" The days rolled into weeks as we settled into a routine of daily walks and weekly food shops. I was grateful to my dad who started painting walls and doors and looking for any jobs to keep him busy. The garden was getting some much needed TLC, and with the weather being so amazing we spent a lot of time out there.

As a family we would gather every Sunday round the table, we would all bring something from our week, whether it was a concern or a fear or a song we had heard and felt God speak through, as we all hear God in different ways it was great to hear each other's hearts. We would then pray together as a family; this was a time we will be forever grateful for as we grew so much as a family and in our faith in the toughest times we as a generation have ever lived through as a country. We embraced the new normal, as churches closed a lot of them moved online, and I was really enjoying engaging with many of other churches out there. My all-time favourite was Glasgow Prophetic Centre, who had their weekly Power Hour slots. This was great teaching and had and some of my friends and I gripped, we would spend many a face time discussing the latest slots, we all got so much out of them! One week they were speaking about the heart and Emma Stark said "ask your heart how is it doing", this was a question that I did not realise at the time would catapult me on a journey down a very painful road, but one I am glad I asked none the less. Ricky and I were also trying to carve out some time together. With Hannah back home now saving for her wedding and with my parents living with us the house was busy so it was hard to get some alone time even if it was just to find out how each other was doing. So we started a wee study on marriage, we met in Ricky's office each day. Through this study God started to deal with the foundations in our marriage, we have a good one but he had highlighted some things we needed to address. One morning as we were reading the verse for that day in john 8 31-32 where Jesus said, "if you hold to my teaching you are really my disciples, then you will know the truth and the truth will set you free." Due to me asking the question "heart how are you?"I started crying and said to Ricky "I don't feel free!!" We reached out at this time to a couple from Glasgow whom we had known for many years through our church. We started meeting with them on a monthly basis on zoom as we walked out this journey. We valued their wisdom and experience. We also sought their advice as we prayed together and sensed the time was coming to plant the church that God had laid on our hearts almost ten years previously. But how was that going to look? We were in the middle of a pandemic and the churches were closed! Ricky came up with the idea of 'Sunday Night at the Bains', he suggested we do a short recording each week sharing our lives and our journey in faith through these challenging times. To open up our home and welcome in those who have never considered God or what living a life of faith looks like. To be transparent and open, sharing how we as a family were managing and navigating these days with God and our faith. I remember the first week we recorded I cried and said "Ricky I don't think I can do it!!" I struggled and fear gripped me, but as we prayed together, I knew it was just my nerves about making ourselves vulnerable in front of people, but ultimately my heart to show people who God is to us was greater than the fear of what people would say. We had an overwhelming response and I actually really loved the questions and conversations with people on the back of these wee clips, many people would stop Ricky and I if we were out walking or they would send messages with questions or comments on how much these clips helped them.

My parents ended up living with us for ten weeks, and as we started to come out of the first lockdown we were able to help them move into their new home. It was so weird not having them there but at the same time lovely to get our house back to normal, well whatever normal was in the crazy days we were living through. I had been speaking to God a lot about it since I had asked the question" heart how are you?" My heart was still in a bit of a spin, and I wasn't sure why I was feeling the way I did. I put a lot of it down to Hannah getting married and I was feeling emotional about that, I was also out of sorts due to the Covid times we were living in but I knew that much deeper, there was something just not right.

God had spoken to me years ago about writing a book but I never really knew where to start and I always made the excuse that I am not good with written work so this was surely not something I would be able to do!! I always had a good reason not to do it, but now the sense of urgency to do so would not go away!! It was time to write my story!!

On the first day as I sat at the computer I started to type out the introduction and the words started to flow, I got rather excited and was laughing nervously to myself, thanking God as I knew this was not something I could do under my own steam! As I finished the first chapter I was beside myself with how quickly it had started to flow!! But, I had a real disappointment, as for several weeks I could not get past the first chapter!! This one day I sat at the computer and was praying "Lord you said I was to write a book, why is it not flowing anymore?" I clearly heard "you have a choice, you can write the glossy version or the truth!!" I closed the computer down and went for a walk as I knew this was a turning point for me. What I am about to tell you and the journey I went on was one I never thought I would tell anyone, let alone write it in a book. But to understand who Jesus is to me I needed to go on this journey for you all to see the missing piece in my story and to really share the deep place Jesus has in my heart. When he caught it at the age of 13 and filled it with his love my life was forever changed. Over the next few weeks, I walked so close to the still small voice, as I started to become quite overwhelmed, I knew what God was beginning to show me what it was that needed to be addressed, but I was fighting it as I had decided a long time ago I would never tell.

Ricky knew there was something up with me but he was patient as I told him I needed to work things out. My mum who I am extremely close to also started to sense there was something up with me but at this point I did not have the words to explain. One morning I put my feet on the floor as I woke up and I heard, "I am dealing with your emotions". I thought to myself "thank goodness!!" I have often felt completely misunderstood when it came to my emotions. I am what you would call a woman who wears her heart on her sleeve and part of the cost of that was that I would cry a lot! Or so I thought that was the reason why!! I have had many people over the years comment on my emotions and one time someone actually gave me the advice that if I wanted to become a good leader I would need to hide my emotions and not even let them flicker in my eyes. I was able to say "I am sorry but that is not who I am and not who God made me to be." I have connected with many people over the years through being myself, tears and all, and in turn created a safe place for others to do the same. I value people who are real and genuine. I believe now more than ever that we need to be real in order to combat the crisis surrounding mental health, in my opinion the root of this is, not having an understanding who we were created to be, identity is so important and there are so many things out there to give us a false sense of identity. There are times over the years I have felt the battle for my own identity but God has been training me in the secret place for some time, I now know who I am and I know he has shaped my heart to love at all costs. But over the years this has been lost in translation as I tried to communicate, as at times my emotions would get in the way. So I was grateful God was dealing with them now!! When God told me He was going to deal with my emotions, I waited for some big revelation but all he said was" start taking showers!!" A weird request I thought!! Lord you know I love my baths, but He made it clear, time to shower.

Meanwhile, life was trundling along, busy and full, and as God was showing me how to negotiate this season while listening to what my heart was saying and navigating everyday life, He spoke to me about Google Maps. I use them a lot, as living out in the country, anytime I need to head out to drop kids off someplace new I need to look on Maps. Typing in the address and tapping on the street where the house is, I zoom in to having a look around the area, and then I zoom out to see the bigger picture of how to get there. I saw clearly this was like my heart; I could zoom in as the Holy Spirit lit up the area He wanted me to deal with, then while walking about my everyday life I could zoom out and see the bigger picture of where it was all going. As the days and weeks unfolded, and the pain I had buried deep in my heart started to come to the surface this revelation was a great way of helping me deal with everyday life. Which was just as well as our daughter was getting married and her older sister had just got engaged. My poor mother's heart was taking a pounding, but the deep faith and trust I had in God carried me through. The intensity of the emotions some days took my breath away and yes the showers were helping, in there I could cry and let out the pain and no one heard but God. I would come out feeling refreshed and ready to start my day!!

Hannah and Pauls wedding was amazing, such a beautiful day with only twenty people there. It was so intimate; you could feel the love and tangible presence of God. It was also a lot of fun!! We had all been in lockdown for so long; it felt amazing to all be in the same house having a weekend together in such a beautiful location. My heart was full of love and as I pushed into the familiar peace and the love Jesus had for me, I did not miss a single moment of the amazing day, or what He was doing. I had managed to google map out of the pain in my heart and be fully present in the moment.

The turn of the year brought another National lockdown, with the bleakness of winter and the freezing temperatures; it didn't make for such a fun a lockdown as last time!! We live in an old house with stone walls and it's hard to heat! We have two sitting rooms, one of which is upstairs with an open coal fire; this became our room to gather in as a family. Whoever was up first would light the fire and make the room all cosy. We would watch films; play cards or monopoly and often Rachel would play her guitar and sing. I even started doing jigsaws, I hadn't done one in years, but I found them really helpful as they helped my mind as I was worked through the stuff that was going on in my heart. Even through the simple act of putting a jigsaw together, I would hear the still voice as I was stuck on a section of the puzzle, "get up and walk away," so, I did, as I cleared my head did something different, and then came back to it later. It seemed clearer and I was able to finish the section. I became frustrated with one of the jigsaws and I was about to break it up and put it back in the box, (I had got it second hand I was thinking this is not working there must be pieces missing!!) Again I heard " get up higher," frustrated I got off the floor and sat up on the sofa, and as I drank my tea I looked down at the puzzle, and to my amazement I saw clearly, the puzzle was put together wrong!! I had the wrong pieces in place, as I flipped them over the jigsaw now made sense!! And I was able to finish it. Getting a different vantage point can help us see things differently, and these simple lessons while doing the jigsaws, are now key in the way I think!! Sometimes you just must walk away and come back to things later with fresh eyes or look at the situation from a different vantage point!! And to write this book that is exactly what I had to do.

CHAPTER 12

BACK TO THE SHACK!!

Standing in the shower one morning as the hot water ran over my face, I whispered into the water "it was not ok," my voice barely there, but as I said it again, the words formed more and more, as they left my mouth I felt the sobs start to rise. I was now screaming "it was not ok!!!" My body was now shaking with the sobbing as I stood under the shower. As I waited for it to pass, I let the heat of the water wash over me and as the sobs started to slow I whispered again "I was a little girl it was not ok" and again I let the sobbing rise up and again I began to scream "I was a little girl it was not ok!" I'm not sure how long I stood in the shower for that day, but as I came out and got ready for the day ahead, I knew it was time to tell.

I messaged a trusted friend and explained to her that I had something I needed help and prayer with and could she organise a time for me to come. She quickly got back to me and a time was arranged for the next day. I explained to Ricky I was heading to Lossiemouth for prayer and I really would like it if he could come, Ricky's first response was "Babe I have golf organised." I have learned over the years that men and women think very differently, and in the past I would have protested and had a go at Ricky for not being sensitive to what I was asking him. The reality is men just process things differently from us women!! I told him I understood but this was important, and I would like him to be there, so left it with him as I had already decided in my heart I was going with or without him. A few hour later he said, "I have re arranged I can come with you." As I went to bed that night I put my headphones in as over the past few weeks things had become hard through the night. I had started to listen to 'sleep with the scriptures' this helped me so much to keep my heart focused and I would drift off with the truths of God's Word washing over my mind and heart. The last few weeks had been the most intense of my life and I was now finally going to tell my story.

We got the kids off to school with the instructions that they had to go their Grandparents house afterwards as we had a meeting and would not be back till after dinner. It was a very wet drive up to Lossiemouth, Ricky and I love a road trip and to head out for the day, though this had a slightly different feel to it, but I trusted God was in this and it was time!!

Arriving at my friend's house filled me with peace seeing her beautiful home and knowing it was a home that had been filled with many prayers. There was an atmosphere of faith and love from the minute we walked through the door. As I sat in that living room, these women had no idea of what I was about to tell... and neither did Ricky. As I tried to explain to them what life had been like over the last couple of weeks and what God was saying, I knew it was time to release the pain and the horrors of what happened to me at the age of seven. I told my story of the weekend my parents went away and my brother got to stay with our God parents. I was sent to another family member's house, for what reason I have no idea. But during my stay I was abused by the man of the house, evil touched my world! On the day I was due to go home I asked and pleaded all day "is my mum coming for me yet? Can you call my mum please? Is it time to go home yet?" Eventually the wife phoned my mum, relaying her frustration at my constant whining, she was angry with my mum as she was now late for pick up. By the time she arrived the tension between the two women was tangible and my relief to see my mum was soon quashed as I got into trouble for my bad behaviour. That was the moment where in my little heart my emotions were frozen as I came to the conclusion that what had happened to me was all my fault. It was also the grounds used to shape the lie that my brother got the safe house and I didn't... the start of the lies that formed my thinking around who I was.

As we prayed, I entered the dark shack in my heart that had been shut for almost forty years. I invited Jesus to walk with me, and as I asked "where were you when this happened to me?" I wept, as I stood with Him and He showed me where he had been in the room. I gave over the pain to Him, healing came to my heart and the revelations of the lies that had tried to attach themselves to me over the years fell away as the light had now been brought into the deepest darkest place in my heart. As the ladies sensitively asked the questions to work out what was needed I told for the first and only time, the horrific name my abuser called me. There is power in a name, and this one had haunted me for most of my life. It was finally time to send it back to where it came from as it did not belong to me!! This was such a powerful moment in my life and as I handed the seven year old me back to Jesus, I thanked her for being so brave all these years, she was now free!! I saw her as she skipped away hand in hand with the man that had helped me my whole life, Jesus.

As a young child I had no words to put to what happened to me. It was not until I reached my teenage years that I understood the full extent of the horror of that weekend. Shame hits you like a punch in the guts. I believed if I ever told it would destroy my lovely parents. It was bad enough that I had to go through this pain, so I decided in my heart I would never tell, locking myself into a lie from the pit of hell, that had me trapped with the torment. But by this time the love of Jesus had caught my heart and I was on a journey with him and he held this for me.

I have no idea how long we were in Lossiemouth for as time stood still for me. The room was thick with the presence of God, healing came into the room as I finally shut the door to the shack and locked it, never to return! There was a grace in the room as Ricky was hearing this story for the first time; he was processing what he was hearing. He later told me he had felt such a rush of anger towards the man, but as he sat in the room the peace of God took it away. For me I will be for ever grateful to the lovely ladies in Lossie as they were the safe place that day for me and my husband.

Returning to the shack in my heart was painful but not because of what had happened to me as I had forgiven the actual abuse years ago. As I grew in faith I knew forgiveness was key in all areas of our lives, regardless of what was done to us. Because of my love and faith in Jesus I knew the power of it and saw it in my own life. The man that had caused this against me was part of our family for years, and although he died many years ago, I had the opportunity to visit when he was dying and as he lay on his death bed I whispered to him "I forgive you".

My story is not one of tragedy or even about the abuse but one of victory, of a life lived with a heart full of the love Jesus poured in because I made the choice to open the door to him at the age of 13. As I told my story to my family, who were also going to hear it for the first time, I encouraged them that if they had not already opened the door of their hearts to Jesus, then they would need to in order for Him to catch the pain of what I was about to tell them. The painful part for me was the inner battle I had had for years through my emotions being trapped as a seven-year-old girl. My question was "why had I waited so long to tell?" And this is exactly what I had asked God as I lay in bed one night "why had I waited so long?" God brought me to the story in the bible about the wheat and the weeds, where Jesus said "The kingdom of heaven is like a man who sows good seed in his field and while everyone is sleeping the enemy comes and plants weeds", as the story unfolds the workers see that the weeds are starting to grow, they ask "do you want us to pull them up", the reply was "no! Let them grow along side and at the time of harvest they will be gathered up and burned". You might be reading this and thinking "what does that even mean?" Well, as I look back over my life I see it as being the day I opened my heart to Jesus was when the good seed was planted, but along the way the enemy had also planted weeds. As I walked closely with God over the years, my heart was turned to Him, and as I walked with the effects of trauma, and with the love of God in my heart, I grew stronger. The constant questioning, the journaling, "the why God?", and making choices to believe what God says about me, I grew stronger and stronger. So when I look back, (and its why on the front page of this book the shack has gold ingrained into the wood,) I see the times I chose to turn to Jesus as the gold threads shining through my life as I battled for the truth of who I was. I don't come out of this a victim, although I had to come to terms with the fact I was, but it's a choice whether to stay in that place or keep moving forward. As I told my story the weeds were pulled up and burned in the fire. The story of my life is simple without the love of Jesus catching it and the choices I made to continually throw myself on him for the answers, I know without a shadow of a doubt things could have been very different. If you want to read that Parable you will find it in Mathew 13 24-30

Years ago, while listening to worship music on Alexa, a song came on, as the first note came through the speaker I stopped what I was doing as my spirit leapt! I stood still and listened to the words; tears fell from my eyes, but I wasn't aware of them till the song ended. If ever there was a song to describe my life, this was it. I felt it had been written just for me.

The song is called Goodness of God by Bethel Music and Jenn Johnson

I love you, Lord

For your mercy never fails me

All my days, I've been held in your hands

MY JOURNEY BACK TO THE SHACK

From the moment that I wake up

Until i lay my head

Oh, i will sing of the goodness of God

I love your voice

You have led me through the fire

In darkest night

You were close like no other

I've known you as a father

I've known you as a friend

And i have lived in the goodness of God

If you have never heard this song, ask Alexa to play it now, or Google it!!

I am so grateful for God's grace on my life, as living with trauma buried on the inside causes bad reactions, and I have had many over the years!! I now understand the root of these reactions, they came from the inability to process as I had buried it so deep in my heart, and over the years as I'd ask God questions about myself and "why did I react like that?" Continually going to Him with the questions of" what's wrong with me?" I became stronger as the years passed, as layer by layer God stripped away the lies and my true identity was revealed. I became stronger because of the safety and peace my relationship with God brought me, as it grew bigger and more powerful than the effects of trauma. My journaling, as I poured out my pain from events in my life, was key as I worked out why I had said or done certain things. Or if I was struggling with relationships I would write it all in my journal and by getting it out of my heart it was as if I was speaking to God. I'd shut the journal and leave it with Him; it was my way of keeping a short account before God. My Journaling these days has taken on a new lease of life!!

Before writing this book I went to a writer's class at the Glasgow Prophetic Centre. They encouraged us to look back through our journals and see what God had been speaking to us about, I hadn't done this in years and it was at that point before starting to write this book, I read them. They caught my breath as I said to God "there is so much pain on these pages, what is that all about?" Gods plan was to draw me back to the shack to finally set me free. I now live with no trauma. It has been cast out and burnt up, and now the peace and safety of God fills the void. I am whole and fully healed!!

There is so much about my story that when I look back from a different perspective, it blows me away. I am mostly thankful to my amazing husband for loving that broken part of me well, as he took the brunt of my pain that came out at times through very hurtful statements. We are a firecracker of a couple and that's how God made us. But this was different; he loved me well and became my lightning rod for a season. I am also extremely grateful for the friends who have weathered the storms of life with me. I have a sign in my house that says 'Don't wait for the storms of life to pass learn to dance in the rain' I'm thankful that they danced in the rain with me!!

When the well-meaning Christian right back at the start of our relationship pulled a well-known verse from the Bible about being 'unequally yoked', looked in the natural and sent me that letter, I am thankful that even in my young heart I knew the voice of God. The victory of my of story smashes the lies the enemy had used over my life, as his mocking voice taunted me "could that have been the case? Are you unequally yoked? Is that why you struggle so much?" I can tell you with utter confidence I am completely equally yoked to Ricky Bain!! Our relationship is not perfect, but we serve a perfect God and Ricky is most definitely Gods choice for me. I am so looking forward to the journey ahead as our five miracle children all grow up and fly the nest, and again we become their biggest cheerleaders in life as we encourage them to chase after the freedom in following their unique plan designed by God just for them. As we set our hearts towards the plan God has for our lives, we embrace all that comes our way, the highs even the lows!! The bible is clear when it states in John chapter 16 verse 33, "In this world you will have troubles", but Jesus said "take heart! I have overcome the world!!"

I will spend the rest of my life pushing into the still small voice of God, and I will continue to be a safe place for people as God brings them into my life. I will continue to ask the questions and seek the truth no matter how hard it is, as the truth will always set you free!! We are all on a journey and that journey will one day lead us to the end of our lives, I don't want to get there alone, I want to bring as many people as I can with me into eternity. And i want to have a lot of fun along the way!!

If through me telling my story, you feel you have a secret to tell or you have uttered those words "there must be more than this?" then let me tell you there most definitely is!! Most of my powerful encounters with God have happened while sitting in my Bedroom alone. The same God is sitting with you now as you read; He is not confined to a church building. My prayer is that you open up your heart and the lines of communication with Him and start asking the question "heart, how are you?" Wherever you are at and whatever point in your journey you have reached, know this, God sees you and you are loved.

I want to finish with the words from Psalm 62 verse 8 from The Passion Translation: Join me, everyone!

Trust only in God every moment!! Tell him your troubles and pour out your heart-longings to him believe me when i tell you-He will help you!!

JOANNE BAIN

Joanne lives in Aberdeenshire with her husband Ricky and together they pastor Alford Community Church. They are passionate about serving the community they live in. By being the bridge between the world and the church, they aim to break down the preconceived ideas of what church looks like and show that God is not confined to a building.

If by reading this book you find yourself with questions you can contact Joanne by email:

Joanne.bain@btinternet.com